THE
BEATLES
AND
COUNTRY
Music

Don Cusic

Brackish Publishing
P.O. Box 120751
Nashville, TN 37212

Cover and Interior Layout Design
PricelessDigitalMedia.com

Cover Sketches
Alan Moore Artworks
alan_artworks@bellsouth.net

Production Coordinator
Jim Sharp
Sharp Management

Acknowledgments

First and foremost, I must thank the Mike Curb Family Foundation for funding the Curb Professor of Music Industry History at Belmont University in Nashville, which allows me to do projects like this.

I would like to thank the following for their help in getting this book written. They are: Barry Coburn, Bebe Evans, Bill Lloyd, Bobby Braddock, Charlie Daniels, Danny Ealey, David Briggs, Dixie Gamble, Doug Howard, Duane Eddy, Ernie Winfrey, Harold Bradley, Jeff Jones, Joe Chambers, John Carter Cash, John Salaway, Ken Mansfield, Mark Lewisohn, Mike Janas, Norbert Putnam, Olivia Beaudry, Peter Noone, Richard Courtney, Rose Drake, Fred Cannon, and Shannon McNally.

My only disappointment is that I found the perfect picture for the cover but Apple would not license it. It came from the opening scene of Help! where the Beatles are on a stage with George playing a Gretsch Tennessean guitar and John playing the Gibson acoustic. That was a perfect line-up to show the connection between the Beatles and country music.

Table of Contents

Introduction

The term "country music" carries a lot of baggage for rock fans; it is incredibly popular and consistently unfashionable. For the 60s generation of Baby Boomers it was the music for the un-hip and the un-cool and rock'n'roll fans generally dismissed country music as a music they did not want to be associated with. It wasn't just the music, it was everything associated with the country music culture, from down home cooking to the clothes they wore to a lack of culture, worldliness and sophistication. The self-image of the rock musician — and the rock audience — was young, hip, cool, energetic, rebellious and worldly.

Rock'n'roll is music by and for the young who want to break from the past and create something new. The mid-1950s and 1960s was an era of rebellion, an era where young people demanded a "new" world. It was hip to like rock, it was cool because all your friends — or at least the ones who counted — liked rock and it was un-hip and un-cool to like country music. That was the music of old people, of people stuck in the past who didn't want things to change. Further, it was a music that did not have the energy and vitality of rock. For most young people it was a matter of self-image; country music represented what they didn't want to be, what they rejected, a music for the have-nots. Country music was out of bounds and repulsive if you wanted to be accepted by your peers.

But let's take a look at the music itself.

Country music and R&B developed along separate lines, but there was a strong country influence on early R&B performers for a simple reason: country music was heard on the radio, R&B wasn't. At least there wasn't any great demand until the mid-1950s.

The United States has formatted radio; there's a country station, a rock station, an urban station and down the line. In the rest of the world, people generally don't speak in "genres" because public or state radio, which dominates radio internationally, does not categorize by genres. People will talk about artists, or songs, but they tend to give equal weight to all types of music. If they like a song or artist, they like it; there isn't the self-identification with genre ("I'm a country fan" or "I'm a jazz fan") that most American consumers hold.

The thread of country music winds through the history of American music and that thread dates back to the earliest music from British settlers. It is a music of the working class and remains shunned by elites, but it is a music that marches through the history of American music.

The roots of country music are sunk deep in the British Isles, which consisted of England, Scotland, Ireland and Wales until the twentieth century. Robert Burns may be the first "country" songwriter; his songs like "Flow Gently, Sweet Afton," "Auld Lang Syne," "Annie Laurie" and "Red, Red Rose" can be heard as country songs. By the time he died in 1796, the 37-year old poet had written songs and poems that would last through the ages. "Annie Laurie" was a popular song during the American Civil War and "Auld Lang Syne" is still a New Year's Eve tradition.

Some old songs from the British Isles were performed by country artists. The best example is "Barbara Allen," which was performed by Bradley Kincaid on "The National Barn Dance" in Chicago during the 1920s and 1930s. It was a huge hit and Kincaid performed it numerous times.

It has been established that many songs known in early America were derived from British songs. In 1876, Francis Child, a Harvard Professor, began collecting oral folk songs in the United States and eventually published five volumes of The English and Scottish Ballads. An Englishman, Cecil Sharp, came to the United States during World War I and collected English folk songs in Appalachia. Traveling through the mountains of Virginia, North Carolina, Kentucky and Tennessee with his assistant Maud Karpeles, Sharp collected numerous songs whose roots went back to the British Isles. [1]

Liverpool

Liverpool is a port city and during the early part of the twentieth century a number of sailors and ship workers sailed to the United States, taking passengers and cargo back and forth. The most popular liners were the Cunard ships, whose history dates back to 1839 when Samuel Cunard began carrying mail between Liverpool, Nova Scotia and Boston. In 1870 it was organized as the Cunard Steamship Company, LTD. One of the most famous Cunard ships was the Lusitania, which was carrying American and British passengers when it was sunk by the German Navy in 1915; this was a factor that led to the entry of the United States into World War I.

After World War I the Cunard ships ferried passengers and cargo regularly between Liverpool and New York. In America, British sailors often purchased American goods, including recordings. The country music records the "Cunard Yanks" brought back led to country music finding a loyal audience in Liverpool.

American Record labels RCA, Decca, and Columbia all had licensing agreements with British labels (or British divisions) to release American recordings in the U.K. The most popular country acts before World War II were the singing cowboys, Gene Autry, Roy Rogers and Tex Ritter, whose movies and recordings were regularly seen and heard in Britain; they remained popular after the War as well.

Popular British entertainment was the Music Hall, a variety show akin to vaudeville in the United States, which featured British humor and British songs. Because the Music Hall was uniquely British, it never succeeded with American audiences, although big band and jazz were regularly featured in the Music Halls. American music had long been imported into Great Britain, but it wasn't until rock and roll hit in 1956 that American music really captured British youth. Just prior to rock and roll, skiffle was popular in Britain and this music, akin to American folk music, is one of country music's deep roots.

Led by Elvis Presley, the earliest rock and roll came out of Sun Records in Memphis, Tennessee and it was rockabilly, a music with deep roots in country music. Rockabilly was, essentially, country music on steroids and the earliest performers on Sun, like Elvis, Carl Perkins, Johnny Cash, Roy Orbison and Jerry Lee Lewis, were all "country boys" who grew up listening to the Grand Ole Opry and were familiar with country performers.

Country music, via folk music, country records and rockabilly, arrived in Britain during the formative years of the Beatles. Because Liverpool is a seaport, country music was much more popular there than in urbane London. Later, rhythm and blues, especially from Motown, became popular in England and the Beatles loved and copied R&B records. However, the R&B influences came after their musical foundation had been laid.

When discussing country music it must be remembered that, the United States has "formatted" commercial radio so there are stations identified as "country" stations with artists and songs labeled "country." However, in England, radio is dominated by the BBC which is not formatted into musical genres. They simply play records they like without defining it as a genre. That means that, although the BBC, and English citizens in general, may know and like songs and artists that are labeled "country" in the United States, they are not considered "country" in the U.K.—just good songs and good artists. (The charts in the United States are also formatted by musical genre while the charts in the U.K. are not; it simply lists the most popular songs.)

Beatles and Country Music Fans Surprised

When the Beatles album, *Yesterday and Today,* was released on Capitol in the United States, Beatle fans—as well as country music fans--were shocked to hear a popular country song, "Act Naturally," sung by Ringo Starr. The song had been a hit for Buck Owens in 1963 and that connection to country music may have surprised Beatles fans as well as American country music fans, but it would not have surprised those who knew Ritchie Starkey from his early Liverpool days.

Beatles drummer Ringo Starr, born Richard Starkey, had no interest in music until saw the Gene Autry film, *South of the Border,* where Autry sang the title song while riding a horse.

"My first musical memory was when I was about eight: Gene Autry singing 'South of the Border,'" said Ringo. "That was the first time I really got shivers down my backbone, as they say. He had his three compadres singing, 'Ai, ai, ai ai,' and it was just a thrill to me. Gene Autry has been my hero ever since." This was a "Eureka moment" for him which he never forgot, naming Autry as "The most significant musical force in my life." [2]

"I always loved country-and-western; a lot of it was around from the guys in the navy," said Ringo. "I'd go to parties and they'd be putting on Hank Williams, Hank Snow and all those country acts. I still love country music....Frankie Laine was probably my biggest hero around 1956—and I also liked Bill Haley." [3]

Ringo recounted that he lost his virginity as a teenager while "Ghost Riders in the Sky" by Frankie Laine was playing. [4]

From this point forward, young Ritchie Starkey was a fan of singing cowboys and country music and he had a close friend, Roy Trafford, who also loved country music and purchased country records.

"It was Ringo who introduced us to old country-and-western; Jimmie Rodgers and those kinds of people," remembered Paul McCartney. "Ringo had quite a good collection of that." [5]

George Harrison, lead guitarist for the Beatles, was also influenced by country music and country performers. The first record that intrigued him because it featured a guitar was "Waiting for a Train" b/w "Blue Yodel No. 4" ("California Blues")" by Jimmie Rodgers, The Singing Brakeman. [6] George's father, Harry Harrison, had been a seaman, serving as a steward on the White Star Line and first visited the United States in 1927. Harrison worked on the White Star Line until 1936; this is how the Harrison household came to own the Jimmie Rodgers recording.

"My Dad had bought a wind-up gramophone in New York when he was a seaman and had brought it back on the ship," remembered Harrison. "He'd also brought some records from America, including one by Jimmie Rodgers, 'The Singing Brakeman.' He was Hank Williams's favourite singer and the first country singer that I ever heard. He had a lot of tunes such as 'Waiting For a Train,' 'Blue Yodel '94,' and "Blue Yodel 13.' The one that my Dad had was 'Waiting For a Train,' that led me to the guitar." [7]

The Harrison household owned a number of records, including those by Hank Williams, Hoagy Carmichael, Josh White, the Ink Spots and George Formby, an English star of Music Halls and films. Louise Harrison remembered there was a record of "Sixteen Tons" by Tennessee Ernie Ford in their home when she was growing up. [8]

Slim Whitman

Slim Whitman was an American country singer who was a pioneer in bringing country music to Europe after World War II. Although he had a series of chart records on the *Billboard* country chart in America, Whitman was more popular in England where, in 1955, his single "Rose Marie" reached number one on the pop chart and held the record for most weeks at number one for 36 years. His follow-up, "Indian Love Call," also released in 1955, was a hit in the U.K. [1] Both of those songs came from the 1936 movie musical, *Rose Marie*, starring Jeanette MacDonald and Nelson Eddy.

George Harrison's mother, Louise, purchased both "Rose Marie" and "Indian Love Call" by Whitman in a Liverpool record shop. The first time George Harrison saw a guitar was when he saw Slim Whitman—either in a print advertisement or on television— holding one. After he saw Whitman and his guitar, "he knew instantly he had to have one." [2]

Slim Whitman was right handed but played the guitar left handed because the second finger on his left hand—the hand that forms chords—was almost gone, the result of an accident. In July, 1957, Paul McCartney obtained his first guitar. McCartney is left-handed, which caused problems as he endeavored to play until he saw a picture of Whitman, in either the *New Music Express* (NME) or *Melody Maker*, advertising his album, *Slim Whitman and His Singing Guitar*. In the picture, Whitman is shown playing the guitar left-handed and McCartney, seeing this photo of Whitman, took the strings off his new guitar and reversed them so they fit a lefty. [3]

Country music was a lesser influence on John Lennon, although he remembered "the first guitar I ever saw. It belonged to a guy in a cowboy suit in a province of Liverpool, with stars and a cowboy hat and a big Dobro. They were real cowboys, and they took it seriously. There had been cowboys long before there was rock'n'roll." Lennon never forgot the cowboy "with his Hawaiian guitar…He had the full gear on.'" [4]

As they grew into their teen years, country songs and albums were important to Ringo/Ritchie, who regularly sang the old Hank Snow hit, "Nobody's Child" at family parties when he was around 15. "Everybody had their party-piece in Liverpool—you had to sing a song!," stated Ringo. "My mother's was 'Little Drummer

Boy,' she would sing it to me and I would sing 'Nobody's Child' to her and she would always cry" [5]

Skiffle

The folk roots of American country music are found in "skiffle" in the U.K. The skiffle craze began in England in 1956 when Lonnie Donegan released "Rock Island Line" on Decca. "Rock Island Line" was originally recorded by folk song collector John Lomax at the Arkansas State Prison in Tucker, Arkansas on September 29, 1934. The song was sung by Kelly Pace, a convict in the prison who reportedly wrote the original version. Blues singer Leadbelly accompanied Lomax on the trip to Arkansas and later took the basic song, re-arranged it, added new lyrics, and recorded it. The Donegan version was released as a single and became a huge hit, reaching number eight on the British pop charts.

"Skiffle enthralled Liverpool audiences," wrote Bob Spitz in his biography of the Beatles, "not because it was new but because it was so unexpectedly familiar. In it, they heard the influence of country-and-western music, which had long enjoyed popularity among sailors and dockhands who trolled the Merseyside wharves." Spitz added, "There was a time, right after the war, when Liverpool was regarded as 'the Nashville of the North' for its rich deposit of attractions; local groups such as Hank Walters and the Dusty Road Ramblers, the Blue Mountain Boys, Johnny Good and His Country Kinfolk, and nearly forty contemporaries performed regularly throughout the 1950s, including the latest country rave as soon as another ship anchored in port. But while country and western had its share of admirers, it was skiffle that created a sensation." [1]

Author Howard Sounes noted that "A large part of the genre's appeal was that you didn't need professional instruments to play it. Ordinary household objects could be used: a wooden tea chest was strung to make a crude bass, a tin washboard became a simple percussion instrument, helping define the rasping, clattering sound of the music. Despite being played on such absurd household items, skiffle could be very exciting." [2]

Although skiffle was akin to "folk music" in the United States, there were some differences. In skiffle, a tea chest bass was used. In American folk music, musicians did not use a tea chest bass; instead, it was primarily acoustic guitars with some groups having a banjo and/or an acoustic bass.

Lonnie Donegan

Lonnie Donegan was born Anthony James Donegan in Glasgow, Scotland in 1931 but grew up in East London. In 1946 Donegan began playing guitar but switched, in 1948, to the banjo when he joined The Chris Barber Jazz Band, which played New Orleans style jazz. Donegan was influenced by jazz he heard on the BBC and by Josh White, who had a record released in England in 1946. In 1949 Donegan was drafted and served two years in the national service; after his release he formed the Tony Donegan Jazz band. His name was changed to "Lonnie" when, during a concert where the act appeared at the Royal Albert Hall in 1952 with American bluesman Lonnie Johnson, the announcer introduced Donegan's group as "The Lonnie Donegan Band." [1]

In 1953 Lonnie Donegan joined the Chris Barber Band as a banjo player. This jazz group played New Orleans style jazz, generally called "Dixieland" or, in England, "traditional" or "trad." The Chris Barber Band embraced skiffle because it was viewed as part of "authentic" American music from the South and believed to be part of the history of jazz in New Orleans. For that reason, the group began doing skiffle in 1954 with Donegan singing and playing guitar.

In July, 1954, Chris Barber (bass), Beryl Bryden (washboard), and Donegan recorded four skiffle songs: "Rock Island Line," "John Henry," "Nobody's Child" and "Wabash Cannonball." The last two songs were never released but the first two were released on a ten inch LP, New Orleans Joys, on Decca; the other six songs on the album were instrumentals. In January, 1956, "Rock Island Line" was released as a 78 single under Donegan's name and reportedly sold over sixty thousand copies.

In the British Music Experience, a museum formerly in London's O2 Center dedicated to British popular music, was a 78 rpm Decca Record of "Rock Island Line" once owned by John Lennon, displayed in an exhibit. [2] Lennon purchased the record ("from old Mrs. Roberts, who owned the village record shop, opposite the baths") and it was the first song Lennon's group learned to play.

Rock Island Line

"Rock Island Line" by Lonnie Donegan was a hit in the United States in 1956; it reached number eight on the *Billboard* Hot 100 chart during that summer and in 1961 Donegan's record, "Does Your Chewing Gum Lose It's Flavor (On the Bedpost Overnight)" reached number five on the American pop chart. [1] Although "Rock

Island Line" was a popular hit in the United States, it did not spark a folk music craze; that happened in 1958 when the Kingston Trio released "Tom Dooley," which won the Grammy for "Best Country and Western Record" on the first Grammys presented in 1958.

In addition to "Rock Island Line," Donegan had a series of skiffle hit singles in 1956 in the U.K.: "Stewball," "Lost John," "Bring a Little Water Sylvie," and "Dead or Alive," In 1957, Donegan's skiffle singles "Don't You Rock Me Daddy-O"(a cover of the Bill Haley record), "Cumberland Gap," "Gamblin' Man," "Puttin' on The Style," "My Dixie Darling" and "Jack O'Diamonds" were all on the British charts. In 1958 Donegan had "The Grand Coolie Dam," "Sally Don't You Grieve," "Betty, Betty, Betty," "Lonesome Traveller," and "Tom Dooley," all on the British charts.

Donegan's biggest skiffle hits came in 1957, around the same time that John Lennon bought a mail-order guitar and decided to form a skiffle group. The group that evolved into the Beatles was originally The Quarry Men, led by John Lennon with some of his school friends.

In Liverpool, 14-year old Paul McCartney saw Donegan perform at the Empire Theatre in November, 1956, only a few days after the death of his mother. Skiffle was immediately appealing to the young McCartney who, up to this point, was learning trumpet. After seeing Lonnie Donegan in Liverpool, McCartney "began clamoring for a guitar." [2]

"Lonnie Donegan had a much bigger influence on British rock bands than he was ever given credit for," said George Harrison. "In the late Fifties, he was virtually the only guitar player that you could see. He was the most successful person, and had the highest profile. He had a great voice, a lot of energy and sang great songs—catchy versions of Leadbelly tunes and things. I loved him. He was a big hero of mine. Everyone got guitars, and formed skiffle bands because of him." [3]

Skiffle and Country Music in Liverpool

The Beatles weren't the only Liverpool group with roots planted in folk or country music. Ringo Starr's former group, Rory Storm and the Hurricanes, started as a skiffle group, and so did Kingsize Taylor and the Dominoes, Gerry and the Pacemakers and other Liverpool groups.

John Lennon noted that "There is the biggest country-and-western following in England in Liverpool, besides London. I heard country-and-western music in Liverpool before I heard rock'n'roll. The people there—the Irish in Ireland are the same—they take their music very seriously. There were established folk, blues and country-and-western clubs in Liverpool before rock'n'roll." [1]

Ringo Starr biographer Adam Clayson noted that there were "regional shades of skiffle, with Merseyside leaning—as might be expected—towards country and western," adding that "there would be more than 40 local cowboy groups operational in what was christened 'the Nashville of the North' by the late 1950s. All looking as if they'd cut their teeth on a branding iron, the likes of Johnny Goode And His Country Kinfolk, Phil Brady and The Ranchers and-still going strong 40 years later—Hank Walters and his Dusty Road Ramblers plundered the North American mother lode, covering all waterfronts from Slim Whitman's falsetto 'sweetcorn' to the hard country of Hank Williams, with its unusual absorption with rhythm." [2]

In his biography of George Harrison, Clayson stated that "Merseyside... had more of a country—and-western bias, which was understandable, because within the area abounded more such artists than anywhere outside Nashville. On any given weekend, you could guarantee that plenty of the 300-odd venues affiliated with the Liverpool Social Clubs Association had booked The Dusty Road Ramblers, The Hillsiders, The Ranchers or any other band from a legion of outfits also playing the kinda music folk like a-tappin' their boot-leather to." [3]

In his Beatles biography, *Tune In: The Beatles: All These Years*, Mark Lewisohn notes, "For a British boy intrigued by American country music, Liverpool certainly was the place to be. Merchant seamen (some known as 'Cunard yanks') were bringing back goods unobtainable in British shops—cowboy boots, hats, jeans and records not issued by the companies in London—and that led to a small but vocal following of country and western (C&W) on Merseyside." [4]

Mark Hagen, an executive producer with the BBC has noted that country music has always been popular in northern England, but not very much in London.

Bill Haley and The Comets

Rock and Roll first hit England in December, 1954 when Bill Haley's "Shake, Rattle and Roll" entered the British pop chart. Haley's "Rock Around the Clock" charted in January, 1955, then was re-released in the Fall. The re-released "Rock Around the Clock" entered the British pop chart in October, 1955 and remained on the chart until late winter, reaching the number one position.

Many rock historians ignore or give little credit to the importance of country music to early rock and roll, preferring instead to emphasize the blues and rhythm and blues roots of rock; however, early rock and roll had deep roots in country music. The prime example is Bill Haley, whose hit, "Rock Around the Clock," is usually considered the official beginning of rock and roll.

Bill Haley grew up in Chester, Pennsylvania and, like Ringo Starr, had Gene Autry as his hero. Haley became a country music disc jockey on WPWA in Chester and formed a band, The Four Aces of Western Swing, that performed locally and recorded for Cowboy Records. Their first record, in 1948, was a cover of the Hank Williams song, "Too Many Parties, Too Many Pals" b/w "Four Leaf Clover Blues." Their second release was a cover of George Morgan's "Candy Kisses" b/w "Tennessee Border," a cover of Red Foley's hit.

Haley changed the name of his band to The Saddlemen and had a string of releases. In 1953 Haley got rid of his sideburns and cowboy hat and renamed his group Bill Haley and the Comets. He signed with Decca Records and recorded "Rock Around the Clock" on April 12, 1954 in New York; he followed that with a recording of the Big Joe Turner song, "Shake, Rattle and Roll" in June. [1]

"Rock Around the Clock" had a huge impact on John, Paul, George and Ringo; it was their first exposure to rock'n'roll.

Elvis Presley

In 1956 Elvis was a phenomenal, cultural shaking hit; that year he sold over ten million records in the United States. His first release in Britain was "Heartbreak Hotel" and it, too, made a huge impact on John, Paul, George and Ringo. When RCA signed Elvis in late 1955, he was signed as a country act to the Nashville division of the label. That led to Elvis recording his first session at the RCA Studios located in Nashville at the Methodist TV, Radio and Film Commission building at 1525 McGavock Street. On that first session Elvis recorded "Heartbreak Hotel," "I Got a Woman" and "Money Honey." The next day he recorded "I'm Counting on You" and "I Was the One." In April, Elvis returned to the Nashville studio and recorded "I Want You, I Need You, I Love You."

Elvis and the white artists who were signed and nurtured by Sam Phillips on Sun Records in Memphis were country artists whose rockabilly sound was on the country charts before their popularity and record sales led major labels to move them over to the pop division.

Elvis first received national attention on *Billboard's* country chart in 1955 and four of his releases on Sun, "Baby Let's Play House," "I'm Left, You're Right, She's Gone," "I Forgot to Remember to Forget" and "Mystery Train" were on the country chart. In 1956, Elvis' first RCA release, "Heartbreak Hotel," was number one on *Billboard's* country chart for 17 weeks; it was followed by a string of songs on the country chart that year:

"I Was the One," "I Want You, I Need You, I Love You" (#1), "My Baby Left Me," "Don't Be Cruel" (#1 for 10 weeks), "Hound Dog" (#1 for 10 weeks), "Anyway You Want Me (That's How I Will Be)," and "Love Me Tender." In 1957, Elvis had "Love Me," "Too Much," "Playing For Keeps," "All Shook Up" (#1), "Teddy Bear" (#1),"Loving You," "Mean Woman Blues," "Jailhouse Rock" (#1), and "Treat Me Nice" on *Billboard's* country chart. Elvis' records consistently appeared on the country as well as Hot 100 in *Billboard* until 1961, when "Are You Lonesome Tonight" appeared; after that, it was not until 1968 when he re-appeared on the country chart.

At the time of his death, Elvis' records were more likely to be played on country radio stations than pop radio. His last single when he was alive, "Way Down," was number one on the *Billboard* country chart but only reached number 18 on the Hot 100. [1]

Carl Perkins, The Everly Brothers & Jerry Lee Lewis

Carl Perkins was on the *Billboard* country chart in 1956 with his Sun releases "Blue Suede Shoes," "Boppin' the Blues," "I'm Sorry, I'm Not Sorry," and "Your True Love." John Lennon loved "Blue Suede Shoes" by Perkins as well as the flip side, "Honey Don't," which he referred to as "crumbly and western." [1]

The Everly Brothers, another major influence on the Beatles has a string of early hits on the country chart, including "Bye Bye Love" (#1 for seven weeks), "Wake Up Little Susie" (#1 for eight weeks), "This Little Girl of Mine," "Should We Tell Him," "All I Have to Do Is Dream" (number #1 for three weeks), "Claudette,"

"Bird Dog" (#1 for six weeks), "Devoted To You," "Problems," "('Til) I Kissed You" and "Ebony Eyes" during the 1957-1961 period. On those early sessions, recorded at RCA Studio B in Nashville, Chet Atkins was the session leader, guiding the other musicians during those recordings.

Jerry Lee Lewis's first release was "Crazy Arms," a cover of the Ray Price hit, that was a regional success for him in 1956. His first national hit, "Whole Lot of Shakin' Going On," was number one on the country chart for two weeks in 1957; "Great Balls of Fire" was also number one for two weeks. In 1958, Lewis had the Hank Williams song, "You Win Again" (#4), "Breathless" (#4), "High School Confidential" (#9)and "I'll Make It All Up to You" (#19) on the *Billboard* country chart.

Lewis ran into controversy during his 1958 British tour when it was discovered that he was married to his 13-year old cousin. That caused him to be blacklisted from radio and television, although he had two country hits in 1961: "What'd I Say" and another Hank Williams song, "Cold Cold Heart." Jerry Lee Lewis's early hits were all on Sun Records, but he made a professional come-back during the late 1960s on the country charts, beginning with "Another Place, Another Time" on Smash Records. After that, he was consistently on the *Billboard* country chart 1968-1989.

Buddy Holly

Buddy Holly was signed to Decca's country division and recorded several songs in Nashville in January, 1956, produced by Owen Bradley at his Nashville studio. Holly had deep roots in country, growing up in Texas during a time when Hank Williams, Lefty Frizzell and Bob Wills provided the repertoire for many young musicians in Lubbock. Owen Bradley had a strong track record of producing hits by Red Foley, Ernest Tubb and Kitty Wells (and later Patsy Cline, Loretta Lynn and Conway Twitty). Decca released two singles from the Nashville sessions, "Blue Days, Black Nights" and "Modern Don Juan" but neither hit. In January, 1957, Decca dropped Holly from its roster but the contract with the singer stated that he could not re-record any of the songs he had done at Decca for another label.

Holly had recorded "That'll Be The Day" in Nashville but the tempo was slower and the key higher than the later release. After leaving Decca, Holly hired Norman Petty as his manager and Petty produced "That'll Be the Day" in his Clovis, New Mexico studio. Since the record could not be released under Holly's name, "The Crickets" were credited as the artist. That record was released on Brunswick, a subsidiary of Decca on May 27, 1957. Holly also signed as a solo artist with Coral Records, another Decca subsidiary.

The title "That'll Be the Day" came from a John Wayne movie, *The Searchers*, directed by John Ford that was released in 1956. Throughout the film Wayne kept saying "that'll be the day," which inspired Holly to write the song. [1]

"That'll Be the Day" by The Crickets was released in the U.K. in September, 1957, came on the British chart and rose to number one, then dropped off and re-entered in January, 1958; it was on the chart a total of 15 weeks. Other records released under "The Crickets" included "Oh Boy," "Maybe Baby," "Think

It Over" and "Love's Made a Fool of You." Records were also released in the U.K. under "Buddy Holly" ("Peggy Sue," "Rave On," "It Doesn't Matter Anymore"—which reached number one) but it was "The Crickets who had the greatest influence on young British groups.

"Buddy Holly was completely different," said Paul McCartney. "he...introduced us to the country-music scene." [2]

"That'll Be the Day" "was as much a sensation among British boys as anything by Elvis Presley or Little Richard," said Mark Lewisohn in his book, *Tune In*. "If one can nail down a specific moment that the white pop group business—the whole rock band industry—kicked off in Britain, it was when the needle dropped into the first groove of 'That'll Be the Day' and boys were grabbed by its distinctive ringing guitar intro. The record came at the perfect time, just when skiffle was fading, limited by sameness of repertoire and sound." He continued, "The Crickets were so much bigger in Britain...The only group of note was the Coasters...just vocalists with session musicians. The Crickets were another kind of group: vocals, electric guitar, bass, drums. When thousands of skifflers heard 'That'll Be the Day,' those eternally uplifting two minutes, they were converted. It was like a well-drilled, willing and equipped army being given a new battle plan."

"Buddy Holly wasn't pure rock and roll, nor was he rhythm and blues, he was country and western with a beat," continued Lewisohn. "Holly, Carl Perkins, Jerry Lee Lewis and sometimes Elvis were all showing that rock could be country too." [3]

Country Influences on the Young Beatles

Those hits, many of them released in Britain, came during a formative period in the lives of the future Beatles; at the beginning of 1958 John Lennon and Ritchie Starkey were both 17, Paul McCartney was 15 and George Harrison was 14.

In their homes the future Beatles heard a good amount of country music.

"I listen[ed] to country music," said John Lennon. "I started imitating Hank Williams when I was fifteen before I could play the guitar—although a friend had one. I used to go round to his house, because he had the record-player and we sang all of that Lonnie Donegan stuff and Hank Williams. He had all the records. 'Honky Tonk Blues' is the one I used to do. Presley was country, country-rock. Carl Perkins was really country, just with more backbeat." [1]

Lennon would "hold the instrument while he sang, performing 'Honky Tonk Blues' into the fireplace." [2]

Paul McCartney and a friend often sang the Marty Robbins hit, "White Sport Coat" (McCartney owned a white sports coat at the time). Robbins began his chart records career in 1952 with a string of country hits then, in 1956, had a crossover hit with "Singing The Blues" (#1 on the country chart for 13 weeks) and followed that with a series of records that landed on both the *Billboard* Hot 100 and their country chart: "A White Sport Coat (And a Pink Carnation)," "The Story of My Life," "Just Married," and "El Paso," among others before he spent the rest of his career in the country field.

Hank Williams died in 1953, before rock'n'roll hit the scene but a number of his country hits had a strong rockabilly feel. "Move It On Over," "Honky Tonkin,'" "I'm A Long Gone Daddy," "Lovesick Blues," "Mind Your Own Business," "My Bucket's Got a Hole In It," "Long Gone Lonesome Blues," "Why Don't You Love Me," "Nobody's Lonesome For Me," "Hey Good Lookin'" and a number of others might have been considered early rock'n'roll if they had been released in the late 1950s.

From Skiffle to Rockabilly

Future Beatles John, Paul and George first gravitated to skiffle; it was easy to play and skiffle songs were among the first they performed as each learned the guitar. However, by the end of 1957, early rock'n'roll, particularly recordings made by Elvis, Carl Perkins, the Everly Brothers and Buddy Holly, were their major musical inspiration.

John Lennon had originally formed his skiffle group with school friends; along the way, he invited Paul McCartney and George Harrison to join. The Quarry Men obtained a manager, Nigel Walley, a school friend of John's, before Paul and George joined. Walley had 50 business cards printed that announced:

Country-Western-Rock'n'Roll-Skiffle

The Quarry Men

Open for engagements

Leosdene, Vale Road, Woolton, Liverpool [1]

Rory Storm and Ringo

In 1959, Rory Storm's group, with Ritchie Starkey as drummer, began performing at the Casbah, a local coffee house where the Quarry Men also performed. Al Caldwell changed his name first to Jett Storm and then to Rory Storm and the Hurricanes. There was a western flavor in the group. Caldwell stated that "Rory" came from London rocker Rory Blackwell but Rory Calhoun was an American actor famous for western roles, particularly in the TV series "The Texan."

Guitarist Johnny Byrne became Johnny Guitar (which was the name of a 1954 movie directed by Martin Scorsese and starring Joan Crawford and Sterling Hayden) and Ritchie Starkey, known as "Rings" because he wore three rings on his fingers, became "Ringo." The "Ringo" name may also be attributed to Johnny Ringo, an outlaw possibly killed by Wyatt Earp, and Johnny Ringo was the name of John Wayne's character in the film *Stagecoach*.

Influential Rock'n'Roll Records

Author Mark Lewisohn has traced influential records that John, Paul and George acquired and noted that John loved an LP *Johnny Burnette and the Rock'n'Roll Trio*. The trio consisted of Johnny Burnette on rhythm guitar, his brother Dorsey on bass, and Paul Burlison on electric lead guitar. The album was produced by Owen Bradley at the Bradley Recording Studio (known as the Quonset Hut) in Nashville and released in the U.K. in 1957. On that album, in addition to the trio, Nashville session musicians Buddy Harman Jr. (drums), Owen Bradley (piano); Grady Martin (guitar) and the Anita Kerr Singers (background vocals) were on *The Rock'n'Roll Trio* album. Grady Martin played lead guitar on that album.

Another important album was *Dance Album* by Carl Perkins, released in late 1959 on London Records (Sun Records had an agreement with the London label for U.K. releases) which featured the songs "Blue Suede Shoes," "Honey Don't," "Movie Magg," "Your True Love," "Matchbox," "Sure to Fall," "Only You," "Tennessee," "Gone Gone Gone," "Wrong Yo Yo," "Boppin' the Blues" and "Everybody's Trying to Be My Baby." Lewisohn noted that "This was country music with a backbeat, the genuine slapback Sun sound from Memphis, right up their collective alley. [1]

Becoming The Beatles

The Beatles story has been told often and much better than this brief book emphasizing their connection to country music. However, I will give a truncated overview of the career of the Beatles in order to illustrate and put into context their connections to country music.

The group comprised of John Lennon, Paul McCartney and George Harrison evolved through several names ("Johnny and the Moon Dogs" and "The Silver Beatles") until they settled on The Beatles, a name derived from Buddy Holly's group, The Crickets. George and Paul bought electric pick-ups for their guitars and they became a 1950s cover band. They backed singer Johnny Gentle on a Scotland tour and had several drummers (Tommy Moore, Norman Chapman) play with them for short stints until Pete Best joined, just before they headed to Hamburg, Germany in August, 1960 to perform at the Kaiserkeller, a club in the red light district. They added a bass player, Stuart Sutcliffe, before their trip and performed in Hamburg until December of that year.

Before they returned to Hamburg in Spring, 1961, they played at the Cavern Club on Matthew Street in Liverpool, which became their base in Liverpool; their first appearance was on February 9, 1961. They eventually performed at the Cavern Club 292 times and a list of songs, compiled by an early Beatles fan, show an impressive range of songs, including country songs, in their repertoire.

In addition to numbers by Little Richard, Chuck Berry and other R&B artists, the Beatles did Hank Williams' "Hey Good Lookin'" (sung by George), Carl Perkins' "Matchbox" and "Lend Me Your Comb," "Red Hot," (which had been released on Sun Records by Billy "The Kid" Emerson and Billy Lee Riley, although the Beatles learned their version from a Ronnie Hawkins record), early Elvis numbers "I Forgot to Remember to Forget," "I'm Gonna Sit Right Down and Cry," "It's Now or Never," "Wooden Heart," and the Frank Ifield hit, "I Remember You." They also did the country sounding "Picture of You" from Joe Brown & The Bruvvers.

First Recordings

The Beatles first recording was an amateur affair done in Liverpool where the group did Buddy Holly's "That'll Be the Day" and a song written by Paul McCartney (credited to Paul and George), "In Spite of All the Danger." Their first professional recording session was on June 22, 1961 in Hamburg, Germany, during the time they performed at the Top Ten Club with Tony Sheridan. During the session they backed Sheridan on "My Bonnie," ("My Bonnie Lies Over the Ocean"); "The Saints," ("The Saints Go Marching In," which had been recorded by Jerry Lee Lewis) "Why" (written by Sheridan); "Take Out Some

Insurance," (originally done by bluesman Jimmy Reed); and the old Hank Snow song, "Nobody's Child," that had been a favorite song of Ringo's. Ringo was not in the group at the time; Pete Best was the drummer. Sheridan played guitar and sang "Nobody's Child" in an imitation Elvis voice, accompanied by McCartney on bass and Pete Best on drums. The Beatles as a group recorded "Ain't She Sweet" and the instrumental "Cry For a Shadow."

The Beatles Story

In November, 1961 The Beatles met Brian Epstein after he heard about the German recordings. Epstein's family owned NEMS, a music store in Liverpool, and he became their manager. Epstein immediately requested an audition with Decca Records for the Beatles.

On January 1, 1962, at the Decca studio in London, they performed 15 songs: "Like Dreamers Do," "Money (That's What I Want)," "Til There Was You," "The Sheik of Araby," "To Know Her Is To Love Her," "Take Good Care of My Baby," "Memphis," "Sure To Fall (In Love With You)," "Hello Little Girl," "Three Cool Cats," "Crying, Waiting, Hoping," "Love Of the Loved," "September In The Rain," "Besame Mucho" and "Searchin.'" Two of those songs are country-oriented: the Carl Perkins song "Sure To Fall (in Love With You)" and Buddy Holly's "Crying, Waiting, Hoping."

The Decca executives turned down the Beatles. In January, 1962, Epstein requested an audition for the Beatles with the BBC.

The Beatles on the BBC

There were three BBC national networks in 1962: the Home Service, the Third Programme and the Light Programme. At first, the BBC ignored rock'n'roll (their charge was "raising public taste") but the Third Programme occasionally played a rock'n'roll song on their program "Two Way Family Favourites." The only alternative for those who wanted to hear rock'n'roll on the radio was Radio Luxemburg, whose AM signal reached England at night, although it faded in and out.

The BBC had a half hour show at five o'clock on weekdays on the Light Programme aimed at young listeners. In February, the Beatles auditioned for Peter Philbeam, the producer of those programs (there was a different name for the program each day) and sang "Hello Little Girl," "Like Dreamers Do" (both written by Lennon-McCartney), "Til There Was You" from the popular musical *The Music Man*, and the Chuck Berry song "Memphis." The Beatles passed the audition and Philbeam noted on the audition form, "An unusual group, not as 'Rocky' as most, more C&W." [1] In March they made their BBC debut at the Manchester facility, singing "Memphis," "Please Mr. Postman" and the Roy Orbison hit, "Dream Baby," written by country music songwriter Cindy Walker. Walker wrote songs for Gene Autry, Bob Wills and His Texas Playboys, Al Dexter, Eddy Arnold, Spade Cooley, Hank Snow, Webb Pierce, Jim Reeves and other country artists. Her song, "You Don't Know Me," written with Eddy Arnold, became a standard and she was elected to the Country Music Hall of Fame in 1997.

The Beatles First Professional British Recordings

During the Spring of 1962 the Beatles obtained a recording contract from Parlophone, a label under the EMI umbrella, and their audition session on June 6 was at the EMI Studio on Abbey Road. During that session, they recorded "Besame Mucho," "Love Me Do," "P.S. I Love You" and "Ask Me Why." The last three were Beatles originals. None were released and another recording session was set for September.

After the first session, George Martin informed Brian Epstein that Pete Best was not acceptable as a drummer for recordings. Bert Kaempfert in Berlin, who recorded them in Hamburg, had told the group the same thing. This, and personal considerations, according to McCartney, led John, Paul and George to dismiss Best and hire Ringo Starr in August, before their next recording session. [1]

During that second recording session, the Beatles recorded "Love Me Do," "P.S. I Love You" both credited to Lennon-McCartney, and "How Do You Do It," a song written by Mitch Murray. Producer George Martin believed the latter song was a hit but the Beatles disliked it, although they recorded it, then requested it not be released and Martin acquiesced. (Martin was correct in believing it was a hit; he produced it on Gerry and the Pacemakers and it reached number one in Britain in the summer of 1963 and number nine in the United States in the summer of 1964.)

The single "Love Me Do," released in October, had staying power, rising to number 17 and remaining on the British chart for 18 weeks, supported by the Beatles constantly touring in England. The success of "Love Me Do" led to a second recording session where they recorded "Please, Please Me," which became their first number one single in Great Britain. This, in turn, led to more touring where the Beatles were met with enthusiastic fans as "Beatlemania" took root in England throughout 1963.

The decision was made for the group to record an album. On Monday, February 11, 1963, the Beatles recorded ten songs between 10 a.m. and 10:45 p.m. They were, in order, "There's a Place," "Seventeen" (later re-named "I Saw Her Standing There"), "A Taste of Honey," "Do You Want to Know a Secret," "Misery," "Hold Me Tight," "Anna (Go To Him)," "Boys," "Chains," "Baby It's You" and "Twist and Shout." [2]

Throughout 1963, the Beatles played live shows and released their second album on November 22 and manager Brian Epstein signed a contract with Ed Sullivan for three appearances on his American television show set for February, 1964.

The Beatles on Capitol

Capitol, the American label for EMI, had the right of first refusal for any product from their British counterparts; however Dick Dexter, head of international A&R for Capitol, turned down every Beatle record offered so the first Beatle singles released in the United States were released on small, independent labels. "From Me to You" and "Please Please Me" were released on Vee Jay and "She Loves You" on Swan. Without adequate promotion, the singles did not make an impact ("From Me To You" was the only one that reached the *Billboard* Hot 100, landing at #106. Del

Shannon's recording of "From Me To You" reached number 77 on the *Billboard* chart in America in the summer of 1963)

During the Fall of 1963, Joseph Lockwood, Chairman of EMI, insisted that Capitol Records release Beatles product, supported by a $50,000 advertising budget.

Capitol had been reluctant to release Beatles product because [1] British releases had proven to be unpopular with American audiences (the biggest pop star in England, Cliff Richard, had failed to break in the United States); and [2] they had a roster of successful acts like Frank Sinatra, Nat King Cole, The Beach Boys, The Kingston Trio and, in their country division, Buck Owens. In short, Capitol had a successful roster and was reluctant to add an act who, they felt, required a lot of work from their promotion and marketing staff in order to obtain any level of success.

Finally, Capitol agreed to release the Beatles current British single, "I Want to Hold Your Hand," which was their sixth British single. On the flip side was "I Saw Her Standing There," recorded for their first album.

Country Sounds on the BBC

The Beatles had proven to be popular with BBC audiences. They appeared on radio in 1963 doing not only their current single but other songs as well, including some they never recorded for EMI. They performed six Carl Perkins songs: "Everybody's Trying to Be My Baby," "Glad All Over," "Honey Don't," "Lend Me Your Comb," "Matchbox," and "Sure to Fall (In Love With You)"; the Buddy Holly songs "Crying, Waiting, Hoping" and "Words of Love"; two old Elvis numbers "I Forgot to Remember to Forget" and "That's All Right (Mama)"; "Lonesome Tears In My Eyes" by Johnny Burnette, "A Picture of You" by Joe Brown and the Bruvvers, "So How Come (No One Loves Me)" by the Everly Brothers, "Memphis" by Chuck Berry, "Nothing Shakin' (But the Leaves on the Trees)" (which later became a country hit by Billy "Crash" Craddock), "Dream Baby" by Roy Orbison and a McCartney song, "I'll Follow the Sun," which has a country tinge.

Country Roots of Beatles Guitars

George Harrison had long dreamed of owning a Gretsch guitar, which was the guitar played by Chet Atkins; Harrison's Chet Atkins albums pictured the Nashville guitarist with a Gretsch.

Harrison and schoolmate, Colin Manley loved to talk about guitars; in fact Manley was one of the best guitarists in Liverpool and "could play Chet Atkins and The Shadows and The Venture, and he showed George a lot of those tricks. He was a big influence on George and his playing." [1] Harrison and Manley attended a concert in Liverpool by Duane Eddy, whose hit, "Rebel Rouser," was a top ten in the United States and was top twenty in the U.K. in 1958. Eddy, who recorded on the Jamie label in the United States, had a string of hits in the U.K. on the London label, including "Cannonball," "Peter Gunn," "Yep!," "Forty Miles of Bad Road," and "Some Kind-A Earthquake," all in 1959. During the concert, Duane Eddy played "Trambone" and announced that it was a Chet Atkins song.

That was the first time 17-year-old George Harrison heard of Chet Atkins so he and Manley searched for recordings by Atkins and obtained a copy of "Trambone." The song was written by

Atkins and released as a single in the United States in 1956 and then on his 1961 album, *Down Home*. Manley remembered "That was it! It was like: how does he do that? So we found out about Chet and just took it from there. We liked some different guitar players but we both loved Chet. George came around to my house a couple of times and we'd listen to Chet and try to work out how he did it." [2]

Duane Eddy and Chet Atkins both played Gretsch guitars, which attracted George Harrison to a Gretsch. He became a long-time fan of the Nashville guitarist and purchased albums by the guitarist until he owned 11 by 1963. Harrison "studied Atkins note by note, and he discovered inversions, realizing how the same chords could be used in other positions." During the time when school boys Harrison and McCartney got together to practice, the two learned a Bach composition played by Atkins, "Courree," which was on Atkins 1957 LP *Hi-Fi in Focus*. [3]

Gretsch Guitars

George Harrison had a life-long love affair with guitars and, during his schoolboy days, often drew pictures of Fender guitars with their unique sleek, curvy shapes in his school notebooks. A fellow student at the Liverpool Institute, Les Chadwick, remembered that he "often discussed guitars with George as they rode the bus into school" and that Harrison was "always enthusing about Atkins, saying he had an uncle who brought the LPs for him from North America." [1]

In 1961 while the Beatles were in Germany, Harrison almost acquired a Fender Stratocaster. Harrison was set to borrow money from Rory Storm for the guitar but Storm was confronted by his band members who challenged him on why he would lend Harrison money when his own guitar player, Ty Brian, needed a guitar. Rory changed his mind, angering Harrison and Lennon, so Brian ended up with the Strat.

Harrison's heart was really with a Gretsch and, in a letter to his long-time friend Arthur Kelly, admitted "the one I want is the Gretsch." [2]

In Liverpool one night in July, 1961 after the group had returned from their second trip to Hamburg, Harrison saw an ad in the "For Sale" section of the *Liverpool Echo* for a Gretsch Duo Jet guitar with an address given. The guitar belonged to Ivan Hayward, a merchant seaman, who had purchased the guitar in New York for about $200 in 1957. Harrison had saved about £75 and went down to look at it. "God knows how I managed to get seventy-five quid together," remembered Harrison. "It seemed like a fortune. I remember having it in my inside pocket, thinking 'I hope nobody mugs me.'" [3]

"Chet Atkins used Gretsch guitars," remembered Harrison. "He always had a different Gretsch in photos on his album covers." [4]

Harrison gave Hayword £70 and signed an IOU for £20 in pencil on the back of the customs bill issued to Hayward when he brought the guitar into England. After promising to return with the remaining £20, Harrison took the guitar but apparently never returned to settle the debt. [5]

Harrison later remembered that "It was my first real American guitar—and I'll tell you, it was second hand, but I polished that thing. I was so proud to own that." Harrison did not have a proper hard shell case for the guitar but took it everywhere he went in a soft carrying bag. Liverpool friend Bernie Boyle remembered that Harrison and his guitar were "inseparable…He took it wherever he went and never left it for a moment." Friends and Beatles fans soon began calling him "George Gretsch." [6] This is the guitar Harrison played during their last appearances at the Cavern and in Hamburg on their last dates there, on their audition with Decca on January 1, 1962 and on their session for Parlophone in June and their recording session in September when they recorded "Love Me Do," "P.S. I Love You," and the unreleased "How Do You Do It."

The Gretsch Duo Jet was first manufactured in 1953 as a competitor to the Gibson Les Paul model. The two looked similar, a single-cutaway, but the Due Jet was not a true solid body; it was semi-solid with "pockets" that were hollow in the body. Harrison's Due Jet had a thin neck and low "action," so it was easy to play with the strings close to the neck. [7]

Chet Atkins and Gretsch Guitars

Chet Atkins obtained his first professional job as a guitarist with WNOX in Knoxville in 1941; when he began he was still playing his Silvertone, a cheap guitar sold by Sears that he'd owned since he was a boy, and a Martin archtop his brother Lowell lent him. He borrowed money to purchase a Gibson flattop for $50 then, in 1943, his brother Jim, who was a member of the Les Paul Trio, gave him a Gibson L-10 that originally belonged to Les Paul. This is the guitar Atkins played on his first recordings. When that guitar was damaged in an accident (Atkins fell on it), he acquired a Gibson L-7 and added an electric pickup to the acoustic guitar. Atkins used both Gibsons, the L-10 and L-7 while he worked for several radio stations and did his earliest recordings for RCA. After he moved to Nashville in 1950, he purchased his dream guitar, a D'Angelico custom made by guitar maker John D'Angelico in Brooklyn, New York.

In 1954, Chet Atkins met Jimmy Webster, a representative of the Gretsch Guitar Company, who solicited him to play a Gretsch. Atkins told him he did not like Gretsch guitars and declined but Webster persisted and offered Atkins the opportunity to design a guitar. This pleased Atkins, who knew that Gibson had a line of guitars with Les Paul's name on them and he wanted a guitar with his name on it as well.

On July 6, 1954, Chet Atkins signed an endorsement agreement with Gretsch and the first Gretsch Chet Atkins Model 6120, a single cutaway hollow body in bright orange, later went on sale.

Gretsch advertised their Chet Atkins guitars in various print publications and the guitar sold well. In 1958, Gretsch developed two more lines of guitars for Atkins. The Country Gentleman was initially a single cutaway hollow body and named after a song Atkins had written. The Tennessean was a single cutaway "economy" model. Both had half moon pearl inlays on the neck. In 1962, the Country Gentleman, a larger guitar than the earlier 6120, became a double cutaway with a thinner body. [1]

During their first American performance on "The Ed Sullivan Show," TV viewers saw a direct connection between the Beatles and country music because lead guitarist George Harrison was playing a Chet Atkins "Country Gentleman" Gretsch guitar. This appearance—as well as pictures of Harrison playing Gretsch guitars (he also played a Tennessean model) caused the sales of Gretsch guitars to skyrocket.

Carl Perkins in England

When the Beatles made their first appearance on "The Ed Sullivan Show" and Beatle songs were all over American radio, Carl Perkins was only vaguely aware of the group because his son, Stan, was a fan. There were echoes of that Sun Sound in the Beatles but Perkins' view was "Them boys could use haircuts." [1]

In March, a month after the Ed Sullivan show appearance, Perkins received a phone call from his Nashville booking agent, Bill Denny, asking if he'd like to do a tour of England with Chuck Berry. Perkins was reluctant; it had been eight years since "Blue Suede Shoes" hit and he wondered if people remembered him; however, since he would tour with Chuck Berry, who had just been released from prison, Perkins, encouraged by his wife, decided to go.

In their early days the Beatles were, essentially, a 1950s cover band and they played early rock songs by artists such as Chuck Berry, the Everly Brothers, and Carl Perkins.

The first Carl Perkins song the Beatles heard was "Blue Suede Shoes," which entered the British charts in mid-May, 1956. Perkins was the rockabilly artist who replaced Elvis at Sun; his first single in America was "Let the Jukebox Keep On Playing" b/w "Gone Gone, Gone," released in 1955, right after Elvis released "Mystery Train" b/w "I Forgot To Remember to Forget"—the last single Elvis released on Sun. Perkins' next singles, all in 1955, were "Movie Magg" b/w "Turn Around," "Blue Suede Shoes" b/w "Honey, Don't" and "Sure To Fall" b/w "Tennessee."

"Blue Suede Shoes" was a massive hit in America in 1956; it entered *Billboard's* country chart in mid-February of that year, ahead of Elvis's, "Heartbreak Hotel." "Blue Suede Shoes" and "Heartbreak Hotel" both reached number one on that chart—but Perkins got there first. On *Billboard's* pop chart, "Blue Suede Shoes" and "Heartbreak Hotel" both entered that chart in the first week in March; Perkins' hit made it to number two. On *Billboard's* Rhythm and Blues chart, "Blue Suede Shoes" reached the number two spot ("Heartbreak Hotel" reached number three) and RCA wondered if they had signed the wrong guy.

On December 4, 1956 Carl Perkins was in the Sun studio recording "Matchbox" when Elvis dropped by. Perkins, Presley, Jerry Lee Lewis and Johnny Cash (who left early) spent about an hour singing together. Billed as "the million dollar quartet" in a newspaper story a day later, the session was un-released for over 30 years.

Carl Perkins had more singles released in 1956: "Boppin' The Blues" b/w "All Mama's Children" and "I'm Sorry, I'm Not Sorry" b/w "Dixie Fried." In early 1957 Sun released "Matchbox" b/w "Your True Love," "Forever Yours" b/w "That's Right," and "Lend Me Your Comb" b/w "Glad All Over." In "Lend Me Your Comb" you can hear the guitar chord run found in the Beatles' "Please Please Me."

Tragedy struck Carl Perkins when his career was at its hottest in 1956. In the early hours of March 21, the Perkins Brothers Band was on their way to an appearance on NBC's "Perry Como Show" when they were in an accident that left Carl with three fractured vertebrae in his neck, a severe concussion, broken collar bone and lacerations all over his body. Carl's brother, Jay, died from that accident. Carl recovered and resumed touring a month later.

Perkins often composed his songs as he sang them. His first records were made in 1955 with him playing a cheap Harmony electric but he found his sound when he acquired a gold top Les Paul Gibson.

In 1958 Perkins signed with Columbia and recorded in Nashville but only two records reached the pop chart. In 1963 he signed with Decca and producer Owen Bradley tried to recapture the Sun magic but, outside of a regional hit, he just didn't have any hits and most of his recordings were unissued. Perkins was drinking heavily and reluctant to be assertive in the studio, letting the producer and studio musicians define his sound. By 1964 Perkins talked about quitting the music business and buying a farm in Jackson, Tennessee, his home town.

Carl Perkins Meets the Beatles

During his three week tour of England, Perkins, backed by the Nashville Teens, a group of young British rockers, played to packed houses and enthusiastic fans. He was on a bill with John Lee Hooker, the Animals, the Swinging Blue Jeans and Kingsize Taylor and the Dominoes at the Hammersmith Odeon where a banner was unfurled that said "Carl Perkins — King of Rock." On another date, a banner hung from the balcony read "Welcome Carl 'Beatle Crusher' Perkins."

On May 22, Decca arranged for Perkins to record in the studio with the Nashville Teens and they recorded "Your True Love," "Blue Suede Shoes," "Big Bad Blues," "Lonely Heart," and

"A Love I'll Never Win." The Nashville Teens were the perfect backing band for Perkins; they had studied his Sun recordings and knew every nuance in the rockabilly playbook.

Decca's British division, Brunswick, released "Big Bad Blues" and "Lonely Heart." On that same day the Beatles were at the EMI Studios recording songs for their *Hard Day's Night* soundtrack. Filming for the movie ended on April 24 and since then the Beatles had performed at the *New Music Express* Annual Poll Winners' All Star Concert, which was filmed for television, taped a TV special, "Around the Beatles," filmed interviews for BBC Scotland, performed on their show "From Us To You" on the BBC's Light Program, taken a short holiday and on May 31 performed seven songs on the BBC show, "Pops Alive" at the Prince of Wales Theatre in London.

After Perkins and Chuck Berry's last concert, they were invited to a post-concert party and the Beatles were scheduled to be there. Perkins and Berry reluctantly accepted the invitation; after five weeks of touring both were anxious to get back home.

At the party, Perkins was introduced to George Harrison who immediately began asking about his Sun records. Asked what key Perkins did "Honey Don't" in, Perkins replied it was "E." Harrison then turned to John Lennon and said, "I told you we weren't doing it right." The Beatles had performed the song in "G" with John initially doing vocals. Asked how he played the intro to the song, Perkins showed him and Harrison took it all in. John Lennon then invited him to their Abbey Road session saying, "You're welcome to come. We'd be honored." [1]

On June 1, the Beatles were set to do three days of recording at the EMI Studio. Starting at 2:30 in the afternoon, they recorded "Matchbox," "I'll Cry Instead" "Slow Down" and "I'll Be Back." With them was Carl Perkins. When he arrived, Perkins sat down beside Ringo, who called him "Mr. Perkins" and asked about the Sun recordings. "Mr. Perkins is my daddy," said Carl. "I wish you'd call me Carl." "This is hard for me to do," replied Ringo, who then asked "Would you care if I sang some of your songs?" "You mean you want me to write you some songs?" asked Carl, who had hoped to pitch one of the songs he'd recorded in England, "Big Bad Blues" to the Beatles.

Ringo paused, then answered, "Well, that would be fine but I really love 'Honey Don't' and 'Matchbox.'" Perkins was enthused and said, "Shoot, man. I'd love it!"

The Beatles did five takes of "Matchbox" then, during the rest of the session recorded "I'll Cry Instead," "Slow Down" and "I'll Be Back."

When Lennon asked "Where did you get the idea for 'Everybody's Trying to Be My Baby?" Perkins replied, "I just said that on stage one night and my brother said, 'That's a song title.'" Harrison then asked, "Then you sat down and wrote it?" and Perkins replied "No. I started singin' it." The Beatles were astonished. "Live? On stage? Without writing it first?" asked George. John then asked, "What about the melody?" and Perkins replied "It came at the same time the words did." [2]

According to Perkins, at three the following morning, he found himself sitting on the floor playing guitar while the four Beatles sat on a couch in a jam session. Perkins was amazed the group knew his old songs. The jam session saw Perkins and the Beatles playing and singing "Blue Suede Shoes," "Honey Don't," "Everybody's Trying to Be My Baby" and "Your True Love."

The Beatles Record Carl Perkins Songs

The Beatles recording of "Matchbox" came out on their *Something New* album in the United State while "Honey Don't" and "Everybody's Trying to Be My Baby," both recorded that fall, were on the *Beatles '65* album. The Beatles performed several other Carl Perkins songs during BBC broadcasts, including "Your True Love," "Sure To Fall," "Lend Me Your Comb" and "Right String, Wrong Yo-Yo."

Carl Perkins came back to the United States a changed man, and Beatles fans learned of the influence of Carl Perkins on the Beatles.

The Beatles never forgot Carl Perkins and that night in the studio began a long-time friendship. The friendship led Paul McCartney to invite Perkins to sing and play on "Get It" on his *Tug of War* album in 1981. In October, 1985 George Harrison was part of the taping of a TV special, "Blue Suede Shoes: A Rockabilly Session with Carl Perkins and Friends." The show aired in January in the U.K. and U.S.; on the show Harrison sang "Everybody's Trying To Be My Baby" and "Glad All Over," did a duet with Perkins on "Your True Love," and played guitar and did backing vocals on "Blue Suede Shoes," "Gone, Gone, Gone," "Whole Lotta Shakin' Goin' On" and a medley that included "That's All Right, Mama," "Blue Moon of Kentucky" and "Night Train to Memphis." The guitar he played was the Gretsch 6120, the first

Gretsch the guitar company made for Chet Atkins. Ringo sang lead on "Honey Don't" and shared the lead vocals on "Matchbox" with Perkins and Eric Clapton. Ringo also played drums during the show. On Perkins' last album, *Go, Cat, Go*, Harrison and Perkins wrote "Distance Makes No Difference With Love."

When Carl Perkins died, on January 19, 1998, George Harrison and his wife Olivia flew to Jackson, Tennessee for his funeral. During the service, Harrison was invited to perform. He got up and, after saying "God Bless Carl Perkins," sang "Your True Love," with an acoustic guitar.

Beatle Guitars & Country Music

The young men (and it was almost exclusively young men) in skiffle groups in England during the 1950s started out with cheap, acoustic guitars. Most, like the Quarry Men, could not afford expensive, top-of-the-line guitars and for those who could afford one, those guitars were difficult to find. The British government blocked imports from the United States from 1951 to 1959 to protect their manufacturing base, so American guitars were generally unavailable to British buyers.

Country music recordings began with "string bands," usually comprised of a fiddle, banjo, guitar and sometimes a bass—all acoustic. Although many early performers played cheap guitars, at the professional level country performers favored either a Gibson or Martin guitar. In the early days of country music, Jimmie Rodgers played a Martin, Maybelle Carter of the Carter Family played a Gibson, Gene Autry played a Martin and so did Roy Rogers when he was a founding member of the Sons of the Pioneers.

Martin Guitars was started by C.F. Martin in 1833; in 1839 C.F. Martin established his factory in Nazareth, Pennsylvania. The earliest Martin guitars were gut string but in 1922 Martin produced a line of guitars with steel strings. During the early 1930s Martin introduced new guitar models which defined the Martin Guitar for years. In late 1929, Martin introduced the 000-28 "Orchestra Model"; the name was soon shortened to OM-28. In 1930, the OM-18, a smaller model made of mahogany, was introduced. The OM models were soon popular with singing cowboys and western swing guitarists. In 1933 Martin built a D-45 especially for Gene Autry; this was the first D-45 ever made.

The Gibson Company was founded in Kalamazoo, Michigan by Orville Gibson. A key figure in the growth of Gibson was Lloyd Loar, who supervised the creation of the L-5. During the early 1920s, an L-5 archtop guitar with a f-hole was developed which Eddie Lang popularized while he accompanied Bing Crosby; in country music, Maybelle Carter performed on an L-5, using the famous "Carter Lick." (The "Carter lick" is a way of strumming the guitar where the thumb plays the bass strings—either a bass line or melody—while the fingers brush the strings for the full chord.)

Between 1924 to 1948, the guitar became the centerpiece for Gibson, replacing the mandolin, and the company created the first archtop guitar. Their ES-150 was the first commercially successful electric guitar and was popularized by jazz guitarist Charlie Christian with the Benny Goodman group.

Radio and recordings played a major role in making the guitar a popular instrument during the 1920s. Recordings of early string bands, led by the fiddle but often accompanied by a guitar, followed. In 1927 in Bristol, Tennessee, the Carter Family, with Maybelle on guitar, Sarah on autoharp and Sarah's husband, A.P. as principal songwriter, recorded several songs for the Victor Company. Jimmie Rodgers, who accompanied himself on guitar, also recorded during those sessions and those acts became two of the most influential acts in early country music. Their recordings were helped by the invention of the microphone, which allowed the guitar to be heard as it accompanied a singer. Prior to this, the banjo was the preferred accompanying instrument because it was louder. [1]

As noted in another section of this book, George Harrison was first attracted to the sound of a guitar when he heard Jimmie Rodgers play his Martin on "Waiting For a Train."

The Beatles and The Singing Cowboys

Guitars were popularized by the Singing Cowboys of the 1930s and 1940s, who generally played a guitar on screen as they sang. The first successful singing cowboy was Gene Autry, who starred in his first feature film, *Tumbling Tumbleweeds*, in 1935. In early 1934, the Sons of the Pioneers was formed; in that group was guitarist Karl Farr and member Roy Rogers also played guitar.

Other singing cowboys followed Autry and the Sons of the Pioneers to the silver screen. Photos of the singing cowboys, especially Gene Autry, Roy Rogers and Tex Ritter, often showed them holding a guitar and in their movies they are often shown playing the guitar as they sing. Young boys and girls watching those movies--or seeing those photos--were inspired to pick up a guitar and learn to play.

The guitar in America became popular with the mass audience because the catalogues—Sears and Montgomery Ward—sold mass manufactured guitars cheaply. One of the most popular was the "Gene Autry Round-Up Guitar" sold by Sears.

Gene Autry and Roy Roger both performed in Liverpool during their career. In the summer of 1939 (before any of the Beatles were born) Autry, with his horse Champion, did a tour of London, Liverpool, Dublin, Glasgow and Danzig. On September 1, 1939 Autry was in Liverpool when Hitler sent his blitzkrieg across the German border into Poland, causing Great Britain and France to declare war on Germany, precipitating World War II.

Roy Rogers did a tour during the winter of 1954 of Glasgow, Edinburgh, Birmingham, Liverpool, Belfast and Dublin. In Liverpool, Roy and Dale Evans were both in bed with pneumonia but had to perform or face a lawsuit; they managed to put on their show with Roy first riding his trusty mount Trigger from the Adelphi Hotel, where they stayed, down Lime Street to the Empire Theatre, where they performed.

(NOTE: When I've been in Liverpool and the subject of Roy Rogers and Trigger came up, I was often told that Trigger died after the Liverpool visit, generally on the boat back to the United States. This is not true; Trigger died on July 3, 1965 at the age of 31—eleven years after his appearances in Liverpool.) [1]

Guitars became identified with performers in country music. During the 1940s when artists such as Ernest Tubb (who played Jimmie Rodgers' Martin), Eddy Arnold (Gibson) and Red Foley (Martin) were seen playing a guitar as they sang; in the 1950s artists such as Ray Price, Lefty Frizzell, Johnny Cash, and Carl Smith all played Gibsons. The guitars of sidemen were important, too. Ernest Tubb's lead guitar player, Billy Byrd, played a Gibson while Nashville sidemen Hank Garland, Grady Martin and Harold Bradley played Gibsons. On the West Coast, Buck Owens and his lead guitar player, Don Rich, both played Fenders.

Early rock'n'roll stars also became identified with their guitars. Elvis Presley played a Martin but his lead guitarist, Scotty Moore, played a Super 400 Gibson. The Everly Brothers played matching Gibsons, Buddy Holly played a Fender and Carl Perkins played a Gibson Les Paul. Duane Eddy and Eddie Cochran played a Gretsch, Gene Vincent played a Gibson while his lead guitarist, Cliff Gallup, played a Fender. Johnny Cash played a Martin while his lead guitarist, Luther Perkins, played a Fender.

Rickenbacker

The first American-made guitar purchased by the Beatles was the Rickenbacker 325 purchased by John Lennon in Hamburg, Germany in November, 1960. The Rickenbacker company, based in Santa Ana, California, was the first to produce an electric guitar in 1932, although it was actually a lap steel guitar (known as "the frying pan").

The Rickenbacker was not a popular guitar amongst country musicians or even Americans; it was almost unheard of until the Beatles hit.

Lennon was attracted to the Rickenbacker because he had seen a picture of Toots Thielemans playing one. Thielemans was a Belgium born jazz musician, known for his whistling and harmonica prowess as well as his guitar playing and was a member of the George Shearing Quintet. Shearing, a British jazz pianist, recorded a "live" album, probably *Shearing on Stage* (1957 on Capitol) that pictured Thielemans on the cover. This guitar became identified with him and the Beatles.

Ironically, in 1964 Chet Atkins recorded a song written by Toots Thieleman, "Bluesette," for his *Progressive Pickin'* album.

The next American-made guitar owned by the Beatles was the Gretsch Duo-Jet, purchased by George Harrison in July, 1961.

Buddy Holly played a Fender Stratocaster and a picture of Holly and his Strat was on the cover of the *Chirping Crickets* album. The Strat became the most wished-for guitar amongst British guitarists. On November 20, 1959 George Harrison purchased a "Futurama" guitar made in Czechoslovakia from Frank Hessy's music store in Liverpool on a hire-purchase agreement. Known in America as the "easy payment plan" or "buying on time," the customer put down a deposit and then made weekly payments. The Futurama wasn't a Stratocaster, but it was the closest a young British guy could get to a Strat at the time. There were three pickups, the action was high (strings were about half an inch above the fret board) and it was difficult to play, but it was as good as Harrison could afford and obtain at the time. George remembered that the Futurama was "a very bad copy of a Fender Stratocaster." [1]

The top of the line American guitars were those made by Gibson, Martin and Fender. In 1960, those guitars began to be imported into Great Britain in limited numbers. However, they were expensive to obtain, and beyond the price range of most British teens. Fender guitars became popular with young British musicians because the guitarist in Cliff Richards' band played a Fender and so did Buddy Holly.

The Beatles and Gibson Guitars

The first direct exposure the Beatles had with Martin and Gibson guitars came in Hamburg when they backed Tony Sheridan. Tony Sheridan played a Martin D-28 flat-top with an electric pickup. He also owned two Gibson ES-175s, electric guitars with one having one pickup and the other having two. The ES-175 was an archtop hollow body electric that jazz players loved. During the Beatles performances in Hamburg, the musicians often traded guitars so the Beatles—particularly Lennon and Harrison— sometimes played Sheridan's guitars. [1]

On the recording session with Sheridan, the singer claimed that Lennon played one of his Gibson ES-175s for their recordings of "Cry For a Shadow" and "Ain't She Sweet."

After their first session for EMI at the Abbey Road studio on September 4, 1962, Lennon and Harrison received a pair of Gibson J-160E guitars (they called them their "jumbo's) they had ordered from a catalogue at Rushworth's music store in Liverpool. The J-160E, a flat top acoustic guitar with a built in electric pickup, was introduced by Gibson in 1954. The guitars Lennon and Harrison purchased were shipped by boat on June 27; it took over two months for them to arrive in Liverpool. Those guitars could be played in hotel rooms or backstage without an amplifier, or could be amplified so they could be heard during their concerts. McCartney, Lennon and Harrison used acoustic guitars to write songs and demonstrate them to other members in the studio. [2]

In early 1963, Lennon and Harrison used their Gibson acoustics plugged into amps on live performances as well as radio and TV appearances on the BBC. For their third single, "From Me To You," both Lennon and Harrison played their Gibsons.

George Harrison and the
Gretsch Country Gentleman

In May, 1963, the Beatles were on a British package tour with Roy Orbison, who played a Gibson. During that time, the Beatles visited the Sound City music store in London on Rupert Street owned by Ivor Arbiter where George Harrison purchased his first Gretsch Chet Atkins Country Gentleman guitar. The Country Gentleman was a double cut-a-way with a Bigsby tailpiece, two pickups and f-holes. Sound City was the exclusive distributor for Gretsch guitars in the U.K. Harrison began using his Gretsch Country Gentleman on radio and TV appearances.

On July 1, 1963 The Beatles recorded "She Loves You" b/w "I'll Get You" and a picture taken that day shows Harrison with his Gretsch Country Gentleman, Lennon with his acoustic Gibson, and McCartney with his Hofner bass.

The Country Line-Up

The line-up of an electric guitar playing lead with an acoustic rhythm guitar is a standard line-up for country music recordings and the Beatles used this line-up for a number of their songs. During their early years, before the group had a regular drummer, they told club owners and others booking them that "the beat is in the rhythm" when confronted with the fact that they didn't have a drummer. Early country recordings also used the rhythm guitar for the "beat" because drums were not used.

The rhythm guitar provided this "beat" through the player's way of strumming, which was a "full" strum, either up and down—playing the chord on both the up and down stroke or by the "pick and strum" method where the player "picks" the bass note, then strums the chord. A rhythm guitarist could also "choke" a chord to create a "sock" rhythm, which consisted of a heavy downward strum, and then raising the chord hand to mute the strings. The Beatles often used the full strum of an acoustic guitar, which they developed from their skiffle days and which is why many of those who heard the early Beatles thought they sounded more "country" than other bands.

Defining Country Music

Country music is defined by its acceptance at country formatted radio stations, in country media and by country fans. If a record is played on country music radio stations, if the artist defines himself/ herself as "country," and is popularized through country music media, then the recording is accepted as "country." In that sense, almost any Beatles song could be considered a "country" song if recorded by a self-defined country artist and played on country radio. Some of their songs fit more easily into this format; however, the Beatles themselves were never considered "country" because they defined themselves as "pop" and "rock." Further, their audience defined themselves at that time as "young" and "pop" or "rock."

The essential difference between the labels of "pop/rock" and country is self-definition and attitude. Pop/rock performers tend to play before young audiences or those who want to be "hip" and "contemporary." Country performers and audiences see themselves as an "every man" and "down home," the "average Joe" rather than belonging to an elite group.

George Harrison's American Visit

Beginning on September 16, 1963, the Beatles took a two week holiday. During this break, George Harrison, with his brother Peter, went to the United States to visit their sister, Louise Harrison Caldwell, who lived at 113 McCann Street in Benton, Illinois. Benton is located in Southern Illinois, about 100 miles east of St. Louis and 90 miles west of Evansville, Indiana, and about 300 miles south southwest of Chicago. Louise and her husband, Gordon, had moved to Benton from Canada in March.

George had written to his sister from the Albany Hotel in Birmingham while the Beatles were on a British tour. In the letter, George asked Louise, "Do you mind if Ringo and I pop over to see you all?" George said he wanted to fly over "to see everybody" and that he might "call in at Nashville for a few days too, to see Roy Orbison...and possibly Chet Atkins, a favourite of mine." [1]

The Harrison brothers flew into Lambert Airport in St. Louis on September, 17; Gordon and Louise and their two children met George and Peter and drove to Benton on Route 3 in their 1961 white Dodge Dart. Louise had not seen her brothers in seven years. The other Beatles had vacationed in Europe: John and Cynthia Lennon in Paris while Paul McCartney and Ringo Starr went to Greece. Ironically, Ringo was originally scheduled to accompany George to the United States until he discovered that

Louise intended to promote them to the media. He then decided against the trip because he wanted to "just get away from it all" and have a simple vacation. [2]

Louise had been actively campaigning to get The Beatles radio airplay. She contacted KXOK in St. Louis and was told the station had been playing Del Shannon's recording of "From Me To You." Bud Connell, program director of KXOK, sent Louise a letter declining to play Beatles records. In England, "She Loves You" was number one but The Beatles had difficulty finding a label to distribute their records, (Capitol, the American label under the EMI umbrella had consistently declined to issue their recordings so "She Loves You" was released on Swan Records, an independent label formed by Dick Clark, Tony Mammarella and Bernie Binnick in 1957 and based in Philadelphia.)

Louise took George to WFRX in West Frankfort, Illinois and the station played some Beatles songs and he was interviewed on the air by Marcia Shafer, a 17-year old high school senior whose father owned the station. Shafer also wrote a story from the interview for her high school newspaper, *The Redbird Notes*.

When they arrived at the station, George and Louise were first met by Art Smith, who sold advertising for the station, and weekend disc jockey Joe Browning. Browning's reaction on meeting the Beatle was "I thought he needed to get a haircut." [3]

Harrison's sister introduced the Beatle to local musician Gabe McCarty, who was in a band, The Four Vests. McCarty had heard the Beatles first British album, *Please Please Me,* when Louise played it for him. Louise introduced McCarty to George who remembered that George "had that big mop of hair, and I wasn't used to seeing something like that. I'd never seen a man with so much hair. Everywhere we went, people stared at him and probably wondered what I was doing with him." [4]

McCarty spent time showing George around the area and took him to the Barton and Collins Furniture Store, which sold records. Harrison bought a stack of records, which included the album *If You Gotta Make a Fool of Somebody* by James Ray. The Beatles had performed "If You Gotta Make a Fool of Somebody" during their days in Germany and at the Cavern; they had found the single in Brian Epstein's record department. Later, as a solo artist, George recorded "Got My Mind Set On You," a cut on the James Ray album and in 1997 listed "If You Gotta Make a Fool of Somebody" as one of his ten favorite songs. [5] Harrison also remembered buying *Green Onions*, the first album by Booker T and the MG's and a Bobby "Blue" Bland album. [6]

During his time there, Harrison asked the store owner as well as others if they had heard of the Beatles; nobody had heard of them.

Harrison told McCarty that he wanted to purchase a Rickenbacker guitar so McCarty took him to Fenton's Music Store, which had the only Rickenbacker franchise in the area. According to McCarty, there were two or three Rickenbackers, all in bright red sunburst. Harrison wanted a black Rickenbacker, possibly because John Lennon had a black Rickenbacker and the guitars would match. Fenton reportedly told Harrison that he could have the guitar finished in black so Harrison purchased the Rickenbacker 425, which was a solid body with a single pickup.

One of the Four Vest's members, Vernon Mitchell, accompanied them to the store.

After purchasing the guitar, the group "had a little jam session of about 45 minutes," said McCarty. Red Fenton played piano, McCarty played bass and Harrison played the Rickenbacker, then left it to be re-finished.

George, McCarty and the Four Vest's lead guitarist, Kenny Welch, jammed at Louise's home and Welch remembered that "The first thing he asked me was did I know an old western swing song called 'San Antonio Rose.' Then he wanted me to play some Chet Atkins stuff." [7]

On Saturday, September 28, the Four Vests played a dance at the VFW. McCarty asked George to sit in with the band for some songs and remembered that he sang "Hank Williams, a song or two by Chuck Berry and Carl Perkins and some slow numbers." The Four Vests, like the early Beatles, were a 1950's cover group so Harrison was aware of most of the songs they played. According to McCarty, his group had worked up some Beatles songs from the *Please Please Me* album and had played them at a previous gig but when Harrison was invited to sit in he "preferred not to do them." Band members later recalled that George "wanted to play some country numbers, one of which was 'Your Cheatin' Heart' by Hank Williams." They also remembered George doing "Roll Over Beethoven" and "Johnny B. Goode" by Chuck Berry and "Everybody's Trying to Be My Baby" and "Matchbox" by Carl Perkins. [8]

On Sunday, September 29, Harrison sat in with the Four Vests at the Boneyard Boccie Ball Club in Benton where they "sort of jammed" for about two hours for a birthday party. The next day, Peter and George—with his new black Rickenbacker--left for New York and then to London, where they arrived on October 3. On that afternoon, The Beatles performed on the BBC show "The Public Ear." On October 5, the Beatles began a three night tour of Scotland, where Harrison played his Rickebacker.

Before their holiday, the Beatles had recorded "I Wanna Be Your Man," "Little Child," "All I've Got to Do," "Not a Second Time," and "Don't Bother Me," the first song Harrison wrote. Two weeks after he returned the group recorded "You Really Got a Hold On Me," "I Want to Hold Your Hand" and "This Boy."

After he came back to England, Harrison only used the Rickenbacker a short while before returning to his Gretsch Country Gentleman.

The Gretsch Country Gentleman and Tennessean

There were two important television appearances the Beatles made during the Fall of 1963: "Val Parnell's Sunday Night at the London Palladium" (seen by 15 million viewers) and the "Royal Command Performance" at the Prince of Wales Theater. Harrison played as Gretsch Country Gentleman on both of those performances.

There were problems with the Country Gentleman for the performance before the Queen and other royalty so Sound City provided a second Country Gentleman while the first was being repaired. This second Country Gentleman became Harrison's favorite. It was almost identical to his first Country Gentleman, colored a dark-brown "mahogany" finish, which led fans to think it was black.

The Beatles often played their Gibsons backstage, where there wasn't an amplifier, and took them home to play as well. On live shows, Lennon usually had the Gibson on stage with him as a back-up in case a string broke on his Rickenbacker electric. This was before the era of "guitar techs" who could quickly change a string if needed.

At the end of 1963 Harrison added another Gretsch to his collection, a Tennessean. The Gretsch Tennessean is a single cutaway guitar in a deep maroon color. In his book, *Beatles Gear,* author Andy Babiuk noted that "From the player's point of view, the Tennessean had single-coil pickups rather than the Gent's humbuckers, providing a more cutting sound," adding that "Harrison used this Gretsch Tennessean on numerous recordings and for live appearances throughout 1964 and then more prominently in 1965." [1]

On "The Ed Sullivan Show" in New York, Harrison played his second Gretsch Country Gentleman with his Tennessean as a spare. During the time they were in New York, Harrison acquired a Rickenbacker 12-string, which he used on a number of Beatles recordings and which gave them a unique sound.

Rickenbacker 12 String

Harrison was ill during the rehearsals for the Sullivan show and remained in his hotel room. Rickenbacker representative Francis Hall met the Beatles during this time and brought along a new Rickenbacker 12 string guitar the company had just developed. Hall, who did not play guitar, was accompanied by Belgian harmonica player and guitarist Toots Thielemans to demonstrate the equipment. The two first met Lennon who, when he saw Toots exclaimed, "Oh, you're the guy." Lennon told them he had purchased his Rickenbacker after he saw a photograph of Thielmans "using my Rickenbacker with the George Shearing Quintet on a live album made in 1955 or so," said Thielmans. "That must have impressed him, because he then said to me in a thick Liverpool accent, 'If it's good enough for George Shearing, it's bloody good enough for me.'"

Lennon played the 12 string, then told Hall and Thielsman they should see Harrison so they went to Harrison's room. Harrison played the guitar and loved it, so Hall gave the Rickenbacker 360-12, one of the first they made, to him. [1]

During the morning rehearsals for "The Ed Sullivan Show" on February 9 Harrison was there. In the afternoon they taped a live performance for their February 23 broadcast: "Twist and Shout," Please Please Me" and "I Want to Hold Your Hand." At 8 p.m. EST on "The Ed Sullivan Show" the Beatles performed before 73 million TV viewers. During the show, which they opened and closed, they played "All My Loving," "Til There Was You," "She Loves You," "I Saw Her Standing There" and "I Want to Hold Your Hand." Harrison used his dark-brown Gretsch Country Gentleman guitar (his second one). Lennon played his '58 black painted Rickenbacker 325 and McCartney his '63 Hofner 500/1 bass.

As the Beatles played before 73 million people in the television audience on that first Sullivan show, "Gretsch, Hofner, Rickebacker and Ludwig could not have asked for a better advertising campaign," noted Babiuk. [2] The group used Vox amplifiers and Ringo played Ludwig drums. Overnight, the Gretsch Country Gentleman became one of the most desired guitars in America. The next day, young guys all over the United States wanted to start a band with Gretsch and Rickebacker guitars, a Hofner bass, Vox amplifiers and Ludwig drums. All of those companies soon had back orders; the demand far exceeded the supply. Country singer Steve Wariner remembered "The Beatles flipped me out too, like everybody else. Not only did I love George Harrison's playing but I loved his playing one of Chet's Gretsches." [3]

During their second appearance on the Sullivan show, on Sunday, February 16 before 70 million viewers The Beatles played "She Loves You," "This Boy," "All My Loving," "I Saw Her Standing There," "From Me To You" and "I Want to Hold Your Hand."

Hard Day's Night

After appearing on "The Ed Sullivan Show" and a short concert tour that included stops in Washington, D.C. and at Carnegie Hall in New York, the Beatles returned to London and began filming their first movie, *A Hard Day's Night* and recorded the soundtrack album.

During the recording of "And I Love Her," Harrison played a Jose Ramirez classical acoustic guitar while Lennon played rhythm on his Gibson. During an interview, Harrison stated that his ambition "was to play classical guitar really well. 'You really have to learn some intricate finger work,' he explained. 'Segovia is a person that I admire very much. He gets more feeling out of his guitar than anyone else I've ever heard. He's fantastic. Chet Atkins is another guitarist that I wish I could imitate at times, but once again he's too intricate for me…My trouble is I don't practice enough. It's not that I don't want to, it's just that I can never find the time.'" [1]

During the film Lennon is seen playing his Gibson on several songs.

Gretsch 12 String

Gretsch wanted to continue their involvement with George Harrison and a custom made 12 string was given to him "but he didn't like it." The guitar was presented to Harrison during a British tour "but that guitar was a dog to play. The neck was too wide and the action was bad. It wasn't like his Rickenbacker, which was almost as easy to play as a six-string." George gave the guitar to another musician. Andy Babiuk noted that Gretsch's representative Jimmie Webster visited England on a promotional tour in 1964 and sought a meeting with Harrison but it never happened. Webster may have wanted to offer Harrison a George Harrison signature guitar. [1] This Gretsch 12-string is on the Chet Atkins album cover of his *Pickin' On The Beatles* album, so Gretsch was intent on marketing it.

When he was asked in 1983 about the Gretsch 12-string on that album cover Chet Atkins could not remember how he acquired it although "I guess the Gretsch people gave it to me." Atkins never recorded with the Gretsch 12-string; he "just used it for the photograph; it was around and the only one handy at the time." [2]

The Beatles and Epiphone Guitars

The Beatles performed a Christmas show in London on December 21, 1967 and shortly before the show Paul McCartney purchased two Epiphone guitars, which McCartney planned to use for songwriting. During rehearsals for the show there were pictures made of McCartney playing an Epiphone Casino ES-230-TD, a right handed hollow body double cutaway electric sunburst guitar that McCartney had strung for a left hander. The second Epiphone McCartney purchased was an acoustic flat top Texan FT-79, which was similar to a Gibson J-45. It was also a right handed guitar that McCartney strung for a left hander. This is the guitar he used when he recorded "Yesterday." [1]

Before World War II, Epiphone was the chief competitor to Gibson; however, the Epiphone company encountered problems after the War and in 1957 Gibson bought the company. During the period 1957-1969, Epiphones were made at the Gibson plant and were nearly identical to the Gibsons manufactured there—same material and same people building them, although the Epiphones cost less. When McCartney purchased the Epiphone Casino, he essentially purchased a Gibson ES 330, and the Epiphone Texan acoustic was essentially a Gibson J-45.

Fender Guitars

Fender guitars were popular during the 1960s, a result of West Coast musicians like the Beach Boys playing them. Buddy Holly played one and Dick Dale pioneered his "surf sound" with a Fender. In England, Cliff Richard's band, The Shadows, played

Fenders. In country music, Buck Owens and the Buckaroos, led by lead guitarist Don Rich, played them.

The development of solid body guitars dates back to Les Paul, who wanted a solid body guitar because the sound on a solid body sustains rather than "decays" like on hollow bodies. He built an instrument he called "The Log" in 1940, which consisted of a guitar made of a solid block of pine wood. Unfortunately, the guitar was too heavy to play comfortably. Les Paul had been trying to develop a solid body electric guitar for a number of years and continued to work towards that end.

In Los Angeles, Paul Bigsby and Leo Fender began to experiment with solid body guitars during the 1940s. Paul Bigsby built a solid body guitar designed by Merle Travis with a headstock that put all the tuning pegs on one side.

Leo Fender designed the first commercially successful solid body guitar in 1946. The guitar had one magnetic pickup and was named the "Esquire." The version with two pickups developed by Fender was called the "Broadcaster"; however, the name was soon changed to the "Telecaster." The "Stratocaster" was developed by Fender in 1954; this guitar contained three pickups and had a contoured body. In 1951 Fender produced the first commercially successful electric bass guitar, the "Fender Precision Bass."

The Beatles and Fender Guitars

Fender guitars were popular with American acts with that solid body sustained, biting sound. During the time they recorded their *Rubber Soul* album, George Harrison and John Lennon sent their roadie, Mal Evans, to a music store to buy some Fender guitars and Evans returned with two pale blue Stratocasters. On the *Rubber Soul* album, Lennon and Harrison used Stratocasters, most prominently on "Nowhere Man" where both played the solo in unison. [1]

"I used a Stratocaster around *Rubber Soul* time, on 'Drive My Car' and those kinds of things," stated Harrison. "I used it quite a lot later when I got into playing slide in the late Sixties and early Seventies." [1]

In his book, *Here There and Everywhere: My Life Recording the Music of The Beatles*, engineer Geoff Emerick states that after recording several Beatles albums, he was promoted to the mastering studio and missed out on engineering the *Help!* and *Rubber Soul* albums. Although those involved in *Help!* were enthusiastic about the album, especially "Yesterday" by McCartney, "there was almost no buzz at all in the Abbey Road corridors about *Rubber Soul*. Though everyone agreed that it had quite a few good songs and a crisp, clean sound, the general feeling among the staff that were working on it was that it was a pleasant diversion into the realm of folk and country music." Emerick added that "Lennon and Harrison especially were heavily into Bob Dylan at this time." [3]

Although Lennon and Harrison used their Fender guitars during the recordings, during their personal appearances, Harrison usually played his Gretsch Tennessean with the Country Gentleman as a spare while Lennon reverted to his Rickenbacker 325. During the film *Help!* Harrison was seen playing his Gretsch Tennessean, on "The Night Before" although on "You're Gonna Lose That Girl" Harrison plays his Country Gentleman while Lennon plays his Gibson J-160E.

Later, during their psychedelic phase, Harrison painted his Fender. "I painted it before we did the 'All You Need Is Love' TV satellite show," said George. "It was powder blue originally. The paint started flaking off immediately. We were painting everything at that time; we were painting our houses, our clothes, our cars, our shop! Everything. In those days day-glo orange and lime paints were very rare, but I discovered where to buy them—very thick rubbery stuff. I got a few different colours and painted the Strat, not very artistically because the paint was just too thick. I had also found out about cellulose paint, which came in a tube with a ball tip, so I filled in the scratch plate with that and drew on the head of the guitar with Patti's sparkly green nail varnish." [4]

Act Naturally

"Act Naturally" was released in the U.K. on *Help!*, the Beatles fifth British album in August, 1965. The American releases were not the same as the British releases; the first American album on Capitol came out after The Beatles had released two albums of 14 songs each in England. Capitol juggled songs previously released in England for American releases, putting only 11 songs on their first four American releases, *Meet The Beatles, The Beatles Second Album, Hard Days Night* and *Something New*.

The basic reason for the reduced number of Beatle songs on American albums was because American mechanical royalties— those monies paid to songwriters and publishers based on the sales of recordings—were two cents a song at the time (now they are 9.1 cents), which meant that adding more songs cost the label additional money. In Britain, the mechanical royalties are based on a percentage of the wholesale cost of the album, so it does not matter how many songs are on a British album because the cost of mechanicals is the same regardless of the number of songs.

"Act Naturally" was recorded by The Beatles on Thursday, June 17, 1965 at Studio Two in EMI's Abbey Road Studios between 4 and 5:30 p.m. The group did 13 takes of the song, with Paul singing the harmony vocal with Ringo while George played lead guitar, before they were satisfied.

The group needed a song by Ringo for this album, since they always included a cut from him on each album. Lennon and McCartney had written a song for him, "If You've Got Trouble" that was recorded on February 18, but the song was rejected because the Beatles felt it was not up to their standards. "Some of them we just couldn't get behind," said McCartney. "I must admit, we didn't really, until later, think of Ringo's songs as seriously as our own. That's not very kind but it's the way it was. Ringo, in fact, had to be persuaded quite heavily to sing." [1]

The Beatles had recorded most of the tracks for their *Help!* album in February, 1965, including some songs that did not end up on the soundtrack. Late that month, the Beatles began filming the movie in the Bahamas; filming continued into March and April and concluded on May 11. The film then went into post-production. After completion of filming, the Beatles went back into the studio to finish recording songs for the soundtrack album.

On Monday, June 14, they recorded "I'm Down," "Yesterday" and "I've Just Seen a Face." The next day they recorded "It's Only Love." On June 17, strings were overdubbed on "Yesterday," then "Act Naturally" was recorded. Ringo had suggested "Husbands and Wives," a hit for Roger Miller or "Act Naturally" but the Beatles recorded his latter suggestion because it was more lively. Ringo was a fan of Buck Owens and that record and, since the group had just finished filming *Help!*, a song that began "They're gonna put me in the movies" seemed appropriate. The song was mixed on Friday, June 18.

"Act Naturally" was the last non-original song the Beatles recorded for an album or single. It was also the first non-original song the Beatles recorded that had never been part of their live act. In his critique of songs The Beatles recorded, Ian Macdonald noted that the group's version "is spritelier than Owens' and contains a humorous touch in the naively assertive bass-drum pushed up in the mix at the end of each middle sixteen. Harrison characteristically sorts out the guitar part into something neater, but McCartney, providing the Nashville harmony to Starr's lead, oddly neglects the chuckling double-time bass-runs which accompany it on the original." [2]

Johnny Russell

The Buck Owens' record released on Capitol—the same label as the Beatles—was written by Johnny Russell, although Voni Morrison's name is listed as co-writer. The idea reportedly came when Russell, a struggling singer and songwriter living in California, had to break a date with a young lady in order to attend a recording session in Los Angeles with some friends. When the young lady asked Russell why he had to break the date, he replied, "They're going to put me in the movies and make a big star out of me." Russell realized he had a good idea for a song so he wrote it.

He could not get it recorded by an artist he was working with and Russell's producer would not allow Russell to record it, believing that songs about movies were not commercial.

Later, Russell worked with Voni Morrison, who had connections with Buck Owens in Bakersfield. She agreed to pitch the song to Owens if she could have co-writer credit; Russell agreed. Owens wanted publishing rights and Russell agreed to that as well; he was happy just to have the song recorded.

Johnny Russell became a popular country artist during the 1970s; his biggest hits were "Catfish John," "The Baptism of Jesse Taylor" and "Red Necks, White Sox and Blue Ribbon Beer."

The Help! Album

The Beatles film *Help!* premiered on July 29 at the London Pavilion cinema on Piccadilly Circus. The *Help!* album, released by Parlophone in the United Kingdom contained 14 songs; the first side of the LP consisted of the seven songs in the movie and the second side had seven additional songs. "Act Naturally" was the first song on the second side of the vinyl album.

The *Help!* album released by Capitol in the United States contained 12 songs, the seven songs sung in the movie while the other five songs were instrumental numbers played as background during the film. Left off the American version, in addition to "Act Naturally," was "It's Only Love," "You Like Me Too Much," "Tell Me What You See," "I've Just Seen a Face," "Yesterday" and "Dizzy Miss Lizzy."

The American *Help!* album was the eighth Beatles album released by Capitol and the tenth Beatles album released in North

America. *Introducing the Beatles* on Vee Jay Records was released ten days before Capitol released their first Beatles album, *Meet the Beatles*. That release happened because Capitol had turned down previous Beatles releases from Parlophone, the Beatles British label, so the British label negotiated with Vee Jay to release 12 of the 14 songs from *Please Please Me*, the debut album of the Beatles in the U.K. The "other" Beatles album released in North America was released by Capitol on the Canadian label Rainbow and titled *Twist and Shout*. That album, a Canadian release, consisted primarily of songs from the *Please Please Me* album released in the U.K. except "I Saw Her Standing There," "Misery" and "Love Me Do" were dropped while "From Me to You" and "She Loves You" were added to make it a 13 song album.

American fans first heard the Beatles do "Act Naturally" during the group's summer, 1965 tour, which began in France, Italy and Spain before they came to the United States in August to open their American tour with a Shea Stadium concert where 55,000 fans watched the Beatles perform for 30 minutes on a package tour. During their show, the Beatles performed "Twist and Shout," "I Feel Fine," "She's a Woman," "Ticket to Ride," "Can't Buy Me Love," "A Hard Day's Night," "Help," "Everybody's Trying to Be My Baby" and "Act Naturally."

Ken Mansfield and The Beatles

In early 1965, Ken Mansfield, who had worked in San Diego with the Saturn and Surveyor space programs, landed a job with Capitol Records in Los Angeles as West Coast District Promotion Manager. This job dealt with artists, radio, television and concerts;

getting records on the air and being the connector between artists and radio station disc jockeys.

On Sunday, August 29, the Beatles came to Los Angeles for two nights of concerts at the Hollywood Bowl. Prior to the first show there was a press conference in Capitol's Studio A where the Beatles fielded questions from the press and were presented Gold Records for their *Help!* album. Ken Mansfield was 27, Ringo Starr was 26, John Lennon was 25, Paul McCartney was 23 and George Harrison was 22 so the young men were all about the same age. The Beatles tended to be surrounded during events like this by "older" men, generally the heads of companies and senior executives. The Beatles were well aware of Los Angeles but needed a local "connection."

The Beatles were seated at the Press Conference with Mansfield on one end and Brian Epstein at the other. The group members immediately began asking Mansfield questions. Lennon asked "Have you ever been to Grauman's Chinese Theater? Are James Dean's prints there?" Harrison asked "How far is Mulholland Drive from here?" McCartney asked, "Gene Vincent was on Capitol — can you get me some of his old records?" And Ringo asked, "Do you know Buck Owens, because I'd like to meet him." [1]

Ken Mansfield and everyone else at Capitol certainly knew Buck Owens; he was "The Beatles of Country Music." Prior to the arrival of the Beatles in 1964, the country division at Capitol "was carrying us through some low sales time," remembered Mansfield. Owens and his Bakersfield cohorts Merle Haggard and Bonnie Owens as well as Nashville's Sonny James were outselling most other Capitol acts. By the time the Beatles held their first L.A.

press conference, Sonny James had 22 chart records for Capitol with his "Young Love" record staying number one on the country chart for nine consecutive weeks in 1957; it also reached number one on the pop chart. [2]

Buck Owens had 24 chart records for Capitol by the time the Beatles arrived with four number ones spending a total of 47 weeks in the number one position. During the time the Beatles dominated the pop charts (1964-1970), Buck Owens had 18 number one records on the country chart that spent a total of 77 weeks in that top position.

A meeting between Ringo Starr and Buck Owens could certainly be arranged; however, it did not happen during the Beatles first trip to Los Angeles because of scheduling conflicts. The Beatles played their two concerts at the Hollywood Bowl, met Elvis and performed two concerts in San Francisco before they headed back to London and began recording songs for their *Rubber Soul* album.

Rubber Soul

In December, 1965, the *Rubber Soul* album was released in both the U.K. and the United States then, six months later, on June 15, 1966, the *Yesterday and Today* album was released in the United States. That album became controversial with its original "butcher" cover (the Beatles were pictured with raw meat and decapitated dolls) before the album was withdrawn by Capitol and a picture of the Beatles with a steamer trunk was substituted.

On the *Yesterday and Today* album released in the United States, "Act Naturally" and "Yesterday" had been on the Beatles UK

Help! album; "Nowhere Man," "What Goes On," "Drive My Car" and "If I Needed Someone" had been on the UK *Rubber Soul* album, and "I'm Only Sleeping," "Doctor Robert" and "And Your Bird Can Sing" were on the upcoming UK *Revolver* album, which was released in August, 1966. "Act Naturally" closes side one of the *Yesterday and Today* album. Ironically, Ringo, who generally sang one song on each Beatles album, had two on this one: "Act Naturally" and "What Goes On," an early Lennon-McCartney song where Ringo has partial writer's credit. There were two songs released as singles in the U.K. but not released on U.K. albums, "Day Tripper" and "We Can Work It Out" included on the American album.

There were a number of Beatle singles that were not released on Beatle albums. The logic for this, from the record label's point of view, was that putting a single on an album caused the consumer to pay twice for the song. Since the singles market was so strong, it was considered only "fair" that the customer should only pay for a song once and assumed that the customer who purchased the album already owned the single. Labels believed that fans preferred singles to albums. This was a period of transition for the rock'n'roll business, which emphasized the single until, led by the Beatles, rock became an album dominated genre during the 1960s.

Nashville Sessions

By the time they recorded their *Help!* album, a Beatles session looked much like a Nashville session. In Nashville, the studio musicians heard a song—that was fully written—for the first time in the studio when it was brought in by the artist or producer.

The musicians listened, then played the song a couple of times, practicing it, and then recorded it. In country music, a three hour session generally meant three or four songs were recorded. The sessions in Nashville were generally scheduled 10 a.m. to 1 p.m., 2 to 5 p.m. and 6 to 9 p.m., although there were also sessions from 10 p.m. to 1 a.m. At Abbey Road, the sessions were scheduled 10:30 a.m. to 1:30 p.m., 2:30 to 5:30 p.m. and 6:30 to 10:30 p.m.

During their early recording sessions, George Martin stated that "I would meet them in the studio to hear a new number. I would perch myself on a high stool, and John and Paul would stand around me with their acoustic guitars and play and sing it—usually without Ringo or George, unless George joined in the harmony. Then I would make suggestions to improve it, and we'd try it again. That's what is known in the business as a 'head arrangement,' and we didn't move out of that pattern until the end of what I call the first era." Martin named "Love Me Do," "Please Please Me," "From Me to You," "She Loves You" and "I Want to Hold Your Hand" as falling into that method of recording.

"There were four musicians—three guitarists and a drummer," continued Martin, "and my role was to make sure that they made a concise, commercial statement. I would make sure that the song ran for approximately two and a half minutes, that it was in the right key for their voices, and that it was tidy, with the right proportion and form. At the beginning, my specialty was the introductions and the endings, and any instrumental passages in the middle." [1]. Martin gave as an example the recording of "Can't Buy Me Love." When McCartney first sang that song for Martin he started with the verse but Martin told him, "We've got to have an introduction, something that catches the ear immediately, a hook. So let's start off with the chorus." [2]

That description by George Martin of an early Beatles recording session could have been said by a country music producer on a country recording session in Nashville during that same period.

Lennon and McCartney often wrote songs separately—or at least had the idea of a song roughed out—before they got together and finished it. The one who had the original idea, or wrote most of the song, sang lead. According to McCartney, during their early recordings the group generally arrived at the studio around 10 a.m., set up their gear and tuned up, then George Martin would say, "Right, chaps, what are you going to do?" During the next 20 minutes or so, "me and John normally would just show everyone what the song was...We never rehearsed. Very, very loose," adding that "we'd been playing so much together as a club act that we just sort of knew it. It would bore us to rehearse too much, we kind of knew the songs. So we'd get quite a lot done at those sessions." [3]

Nashville studio musicians "learned to create instantly," said Norbert Putnam, who became one of the premier studio bass players in Nashville. "There was never a rehearsal for records. Once they handed out the parts, the band played it once or twice and tried to get it and then everybody went on to the next song. Studio musicians have to be incredible sight readers, incredible creators and they have to do this without ever making a mistake. They have to play their solos and parts flawlessly because in those days (the 1960s) we were recording on three track equipment." Putnam continued, "If you wanted to be a first call musician, you needed to be able to listen to a song, write a chart out as it's playing and then put your chart up there and play a great part backing the artist on the first take. If you could do that, you could be a studio guy. If you couldn't do that, you're on the road forever with somebody." [4]

Unlike Nashville session musicians, the Beatles generally took longer to learn a song, playing it over and over until they all knew their parts. However, like Nashville sessions, each Beatle was open to ideas from their producer or other members of the group who made suggestions, tossed around ideas and brought the song to its final shape.

Fuzz Tone

During the *Rubber Soul* sessions The Beatles recorded a George Harrison song, "Think For Yourself" and on that song used a "Fuzz bass." This use of a "fuzz" had its roots in Nashville and country music.

During a recording session for Marty Robbins in 1960 at the Quonset Hut on Music Row, a problem surfaced when one of the pre-amps in the console went out, which caused session guitarist Grady Martin's amplifier to distort and engineer Glen Snoddy was unable to fix it. The song was "Don't Worry 'Bout Me" and producer Owen Bradley decided to use the distortion on the recording. The record was released in 1961 and reached number one on the country chart for ten weeks and number three on the pop chart.

Other artists heard the record and came to the Quonset Hut for that sound. The distortion problem had been solved but another problem was created: How to create and control that distortion. Engineer Snoddy built a guitar pedal with a button that guitarists could press with their foot to change the tone from clean to distorted. Snoddy went to Chicago and met with Gibson president Maurice Berlin and demonstrated his invention. Gibson acquired the patent and named the invention "The Maestro Fuzz-Tone FZ-1" and began marketing it in 1962. Sales were slow at first but in August, 1965, the Rolling Stones released "(I Can't Get No) Satisfaction" with Keith Richards playing the lead guitar hook on the fuzz box. Sales took off after that and Snoddy received royalties for seven years. [1]

The Lost Gretsch

George Harrison's second Gretsch Country Gentleman, a favorite of his and the one he played on "The Ed Sullivan Show" met its fate on December 3, 1965 when the group was on its way to begin their British tour with an opening show in Glasgow, Scotland. Chauffeur Alf Bickness strapped the Gent and a Rickenbacker on back of their car and, just outside of London, passed a large truck. Alerted by another car that something was wrong, Bickness pulled over and discovered the guitars were gone. Back down the road the Country Gentleman was in pieces—smashed beyond repair. The guitar was probably run over by the truck and the group left it in the road. Harrison was disappointed, saying "Some people would say I shouldn't worry because I can buy as many replacement guitars as I want, but you know how it is. I kind of got attached to it." [1]

Cowboy Movie

The Beatles almost had another close connection to country and western music when a film was proposed for them to star in. The film was based on a 1961 novel *A Talent For Loving*, or *The Great Cowboy Race* by Richard Condon (who wrote *The Manchurian Candidate*) was presented to them for the third movie in their contract with United Artists. The plot was based on an actual horse race during the 1870s. A gambler won the bet on the race but the ranch in Mexico he won was cursed, and the only way to get rid of the curse was for the ranch's owner, Don Jose, to marry off his beautiful nymphomaniac daughter, Evaline. In the script the Beatles would have played four pioneers from Liverpool who had come to the American West.

The Beatles rejected the idea for the movie, which was later filmed and released in 1969. *A Talent For Loving* was directed by Richard Quine and starred Richard Widmark, Chaim Topol, Cesar Romaro and Caroline Munro. It was later released on home video as *Gun Crazy* with 15 minutes of the original edited out.

Although the Beatles rejected the idea of playing cowboys, one is left with the question of what The Beatles would have sounded like writing and playing "cowboy" and "western" songs.

The Beatles had also planned to record in Memphis at Sun Studios during 1966 but this, too, never came to fruition.

Country Shipments to Ringo

"Ringo was really into country music," said Ken Mansfield. "I think one reason that Ringo and I hit it off from the beginning was our mutual love for country music. We talked about country music during our conversations and I arranged for every country record that came out on Capitol to be shipped to him in England. I sent them once a month but after a year or so he got in touch with me and said, 'Hey, you gotta stop sending me records because they have to go through customs and I have to go down or send somebody down to sign for them and it's costing me a fortune to pay duty on those things.'" [1]

Revolver

By the time they recorded the sessions for the *Revolver* album, Lennon and Harrison had acquired Epiphone Casino guitars and used them extensively on those sessions. Lennon also used his Gibson J-160E for those sessions while Harrison played his Fender Stratocaster and a Gibson SG, which was a new version of the Gibson Les Paul model, but a double cutaway instead of a single cutaway. The Les Paul model Gibson had become popular with rock musicians and British musicians Eric Clapton and Jeff Beck played them. Harrison's Gibson SG was cherry red and became a Harrison favorite for several years.

The Gretsch Chet Atkins 6120 was the first guitar Gretsch designed and built for Chet Atkins and John Lennon used one of those bright orange models during their April, 1966 sessions when the Beatles recorded "Paperback Writer," although Harrison was also photographed playing it. [1]

During their 1966 World Tour, the Beatles performed "Rock and Roll Music," "She's a Woman," "If I Needed Someone," "Day Tripper," "Baby's In Black," "I Feel Fine," "Yesterday," "I Wanna Be Your Man," "Nowhere Man," "Paperback Writer" and "I'm

Down" with Lennon and Harrison playing their Epiphone Casinos on most songs, although Harrison used a Rickenbacker 12 string on "If I Needed Someone."

During their trip to Rishkesh, India to spend time with the Maharishi, Lennon and McCartney both brought along Martin D-28s and wrote songs using those guitars. (Lennon also used Donovan's Gibson J-45.) Those songs were recorded for *The White Album*. McCartney used his right-handed D-28, strung for a left hander, to record "Blackbird." Lennon, who learned finger style picking from Donovan, wrote "Dear Prudence" and "Julia" finger picking his D-28. McCartney used his Martin for the basic tracks of "Ob-La-Di-Ob-La-Da" while George Harrison wrote and recorded basic tracks for "While My Guitar Gently Weeps" on a Gibson J-200 he had acquired in the United States. (There is speculation that Harrison's J-200 was the same one that Bob Dylan held on the cover of his *Nashville Skyline* album.)

The Gibson J-200

The Gibson J-200 was developed from a request by singing cowboy star Ray Whitley. Whitley, most famous as the writer of Gene Autry's theme song, "Back in the Saddle Again" met Gibson representative Guy Hart and suggested that Gibson build a flat-top guitar that was "fancy" with a larger body to produce a louder sound and deeper tone. Whitley also suggested the guitar should have a shorter neck--12-frets-to-the-body because country singers did not usually play up on the neck.

In December, 1937, Whitley received the first SJ-200 (Super J) after he spent a week at Gibson's factory in Kalamazoo, Michigan, overseeing the development of the guitar. That first SJ-200 had a blonde finish and a 12-fret-to-the-body neck with Whitley's name inlaid in pearl on the headstock. This guitar proved to be popular with the Singing Cowboys, who played them in their films. [1]

Tic Tac Bass

The Beatles acquired a new instrument in late 1968, a six string bass, the Fender VI. Known officially as a "baritone guitar" and informally as a "tic tac bass," it was first developed by the Danelectro Company in the late 1950s. This bass can be tuned like a regular guitar with the heavier strings tuned an octave lower, or it can be tuned a major third, fourth or fifth lower than a regular guitar. Both Lennon and Harrison used this tic tac bass as a bass guitar on a number of songs on *The White Album*.

The "tic tac" was first popularized by the Sons of Adam, a California group and influenced "surfing" music by Dick Dale and the Ventures. In Nashville, the "tic tac" bass was popularized by Nashville session guitarist Harold Bradley who used a Danelectro six-string bass to double or accent the stand-up bass's lines. The electric bass was used in the studio while the "tic tac" was used to add notes or accent certain notes with a "click" sound, produced by playing with a regular pick and doubling the bass lines. Examples of the "tic tac" bass in Nashville recordings can be heard on "Crazy" by Patsy Cline, and numerous recordings of Ernest Tubb, Ray Price and everyone else that Harold Bradley (considered the most recorded guitarist in the recording industry) played on.

On "Rocky Raccoon," Lennon used the Fender VI bass while McCartney played his Martin D-28.

Nashville Studios and The Beatles

A number of recordings that influenced the Beatles were recorded in Nashville studios. Elvis recorded "Heartbreak Hotel" at the RCA Studio on 1525 McGavock Street and, after his release from the Army in 1960, recorded over 260 songs in RCA Studio B. The Everly Brothers recorded their early hits, such as "Bye, Bye Love" and "Wake Up Little Susie," the Browns recorded "The Three Bells," (a favorite song of the Beatles), Don Gibson recorded "I Can't Stop Loving You" and "Oh, Lonesome Me," Skeeter Davis recorded "The End of the World," and Roy Orbison recorded "Only the Lonely" in RCA Studio B.

RCA Studio B (originally known as RCA's Nashville Studio) became known as "B" after a larger studio, known as "A" was opened in 1965. Artists who recorded in that original studio included Chet Atkins, Eddy Arnold, Roger Miller, the Everly Brothers, Roy Orbison, Don Gibson, the Browns, Skeeter Davis, Hank Snow and Jim Reeves.

"Be Bop a Lula" by Gene Vincent was recorded at the Bradley's recording studio. At the time of that recording, the Quonset Hut was used for TV and film production and the recording studio was in the basement of the original building. That's also where Ferlin Husky recorded "Gone" and Johnny Burnette and the Rock'n'Roll Trio recorded their album with Grady Martin playing lead guitar. Buddy Holly also recorded his earliest recordings in the Bradley studio.

Artists who recorded at the Quonset Hut include Brenda Lee, Marty Robbins, Johnny Cash, Sonny James and Johnny Horton.

In Columbia Studio A, located in the same building as the Quonset Hut, Bob Dylan recorded most of *Blonde on Blonde* (all except one song), *John Wesley Harding, Nashville Skyline* and *Self-Portrait*.

Country Fans and the Beatles

Country music fans during the 1960s were not, on the whole, enthralled by the Beatles. To a conservative audience who were a counter to the counterculture of the 1960s, the Beatles represented a culture and society headed in the wrong direction. The long hair, the drugs, the counterculture itself, and then John Lennon's quote "We're more popular than Jesus" meant that the country audience on the whole rejected the Beatles. (There was a Beatles record burning in Nashville after that quote was published.)

During 1964 when the British invasion, led by the Beatles, hit America, the top country songs were "Begging To You" by Marty Robbins, "B.J. The D.J." by Stonewall Jackson, "Saginaw, Michigan" by Lefty Frizzell, "Understand Your Man" by Johnny Cash, "My Heart Skips a Beat," "Together Again" and "I Don't Care (Just as Long As You Love Me)" by Buck Owens, "Dang Me" by Roger Miller, "I Guess I'm Crazy" by Jim Reeves, and "Once a Day" by Connie Smith. Of those songs, only one, "Dang Me" by Roger Miller, crossed over to the pop charts.

During the 1964-1970 period, which was the height of the Beatles fame, the biggest country hits were by artists such as Marty Robbins, Stonewall Jackson, Buck Owens, Roger Miller, Sonny James, Eddy Arnold, Jimmy Dean, Jim Reeves, Little Jimmy Dickens, Glen Campbell, Loretta Lynn, Merle Haggard, George

Jones, Tammy Wynette, Bill Anderson, Johnny Cash, Jeannie C. Riley, Conway Twitty, Jerry Lee Lewis and Charley Pride,

The country charts during the early 1960s were dominated by Buck Owens who had a string of number one singles, including "Love's Gonna Live Here," "My Heart Skips a Beat," "Together Again," "I Don't Care (Just As Long As You Love Me)," "I've Got a Tiger By The Tail," "Before You Go," "Only You (Can Break My Heart)," "Buckaroo," "Waitin' In Your Welfare Line," "Think of Me," "Open Up Your Heart," "Where Does The Good Times Go," "Sam's Place," "Your Tender Loving Care," "How Long Will My Baby Be Gone," "Who's Gonna Mow Your Grass," "Johnny B. Goode," and "Tall Dark Stranger."

Eddy Arnold had an international hit with "Make the World Go Away" and number one hits with "What's He Doing In My World," "I Want To Go With You," "Somebody Like Me," "Lonely Again," "Turn The World Around" and "Then You Can Tell Me Goodbye."

Roger Miller was the country artist with the biggest international impact; his single "King of the Road," released in January, 1965 was a hit in the United States and Great Britain where, for one week, it was number one on the British charts, ahead of "Ticket to Ride" by the Beatles. That same week "King of the Road" received the most airplay on the BBC and sold the most sheet music in Britain.

The Nashville Invasion

There was a "Nashville Invasion" of Britain at the same time there was a British Invasion of America. In Spring, 1965, 30 out of 100 records on the American Pop chart were by British acts, while in England there was a series of albums released on London Records titled *Country Music Who's Who* comprised of recordings leased from Starday. There were also albums from Porter Wagoner, Don Gibson, Ernest Tubb and Roger Miller released in England during this period. There were singles on the British pop chart by Roy Orbison, Roger Miller, Johnny Cash, the Everly Brothers, Elvis Presley and Brenda Lee and two by Jim Reeves—all Nashville-connected acts.

Perhaps the biggest acknowledgement from country music to the Beatles was the Chet Atkins album, *Pickin' On The Beatles*, consisting of instrumental versions of Beatle hits. Released in 1966, it rose to number six on *Billboard's* country chart and was Atkins' most commercially successful album.

Liner notes on the album were written by Beatle George Harrison, who said, "I have appreciated Chet Atkins as a musician since long before the tracks on this album were written; in fact, since I was the ripe young age of seventeen. Since then I have lost count of the number of Chet's albums I have acquired, but I have not been disappointed in any of them."

Harrison continued, "'I'll Cry Instead, She's a Woman and Can't Buy Me Love,' having a country feeling about them, lend themselves perfectly to Chet's own style of picking, which has inspired so many guitarists throughout the world (myself included, but I didn't have enough fingers at the time)." [1]

Paul is Dead Story &
The Country Connection

In 1969, a rumor that "Paul is dead" surfaced in the media.

The story originated with a student who wrote an article for a college newspaper reviewing the *Abbey Road* album which alleged that McCartney was killed in a car crash in 1966 and, since that time, a "stand in" was used to keep the Beatles going. The article was picked up by various college newspapers across the country.

Fred LaBour was the student at the University of Michigan who wrote the article for that school's newspaper, *The Michigan Daily* published on October 12 under the headline, "McCartney Dead: New Evidence Brought to Light." The article alleged that the cover photo of the Beatles crossing Abbey Road was actually a funeral procession. LaBour had a grand time citing "clues" from various Beatles albums that proved McCartney's death. It was intended as a tongue-in-cheek satirical piece but the rumor quickly caught on. On that same day in Cleveland, WKNR-FM disc jockey Russ Gibb learned of the article and its clues and discussed the rumor on the air.

A two hour feature on WKNR-FM, "The Beatle Plot," aired on October 19, 1969, fueling the story, which was then picked up by Roby Yonge, a disc jockey on WABC in New York on October 21 and he discussed the rumor on the air. WABC reached a large audience and the next day the Beatles press office released statements denying the rumor.

Ironically, there is a connection to country music. The writer of that college newspaper article, Fred LaBour, moved to Nashville in the 1970s to pursue a career in music; he played bass in various bands, including Dickey Lee's, and wrote songs. In 1977 LaBour became a member of the western group, Riders in The Sky, who provided the soundtrack to Pixar's *Toy Story 2*, which won a Grammy. The group, with LaBour on bass, also won a Grammy for their album of songs inspired by the film *Monsters, Inc.*

Riders In The Sky are members of the Grand Ole Opry and have been a pivotal group in the resurgence of Western music, bringing back a number of Western classics originally done by the Sons of the Pioneers, Gene Autry and Roy Rogers. Fred LaBour, known as "Too Slim" in the group, has the unique honor of winning two Grammys as well as being a source of the Paul is Dead rumor about multi-Grammy winner Paul McCartney. [1]

The Beatles Last Recordings as a Group

During 1969 the Beatles did their last recordings as a group. On January 2, at Twickenham Film Studios they began rehearsing songs for a television show and arranged for the rehearsals to be filmed. On January 22, they moved to the Apple Studios in the basement of their office building on Saville Row. Billy Preston, who met the Beatles in 1962 in Hamburg when he was part of Little Richard's backing group, stopped by the Saville Row offices and was invited by George Harrison to be part of the sessions. On January 30, they performed "Get Back," "Don't Let Me Down," "I've Got a Feeling," "The One After 909" and "Dig a Pony" on the rooftop of their Saville Row building.

There had been conflicts for quite a while; Ringo had quit the group in August, 1968 but returned; George quit in January,

1969 but also returned. In September, 1969, John told the others he wanted "a divorce."

The Beatles recorded the songs for their *Let It Be* and *Abbey Road* albums throughout 1969 with the last song on the *Let It Be* album, George Harrison's "I, Me, Mine" recorded on January 3, 1970 by George, Paul and Ringo while John was in Denmark on a holiday. Most of the *Let It Be* project had been recorded prior to the *Abbey Road* album, although some songs drifted through both recording projects. The *Let It Be* album and film were not finished until 1970, after producer Phil Spector, brought in by John and George, did edits and overdubbed strings for the album.

In addition to Beatles projects, John Lennon had recorded several albums during 1969, including *Two Virgins* (with the controversial cover photo of John and Yoko standing naked, facing the camera). On March 2, 1969, John and Yoko performed an "experimental music" concert at Cambridge University; the concert consisted of Yoko's vocal gymnastics while John played electric guitar with feedback. A saxophonist and percussionist joined them. An album of this concert, *Unfinished Music No 2: Life With the Lions*, was released on Apple in Britain on May 9.

In September 13, John Lennon performed at the University of Toronto with the Plastic Ono Band for a rock'n'roll revival show. The Plastic Ono Band consisted of Yoko Ono (vocals), Eric Clapton (guitar), Klaus Voormann (bass), Alan White (drums), and John on guitar and vocals. In December, the album, *Live Peace in Toronto 1969* was released; on the album was the Carl Perkins' classic "Blue Suede Shoes."

Part II:
Solo Beatles

Ringo's Sentimental Journey

The first solo musical project recorded by a Beatle was Ringo's *Sentimental Journey*. The project began in October, 1969 and was completed in March, 1970; on March 27, a few weeks after completion, the album was released. On the album were two country songs, "I'm a Fool to Care" and "Have I Told You Lately That I Love You?"

"I'm a Fool to Care" was written by Ted Daffan, who composed the country classics "Born to Lose" and "Truck Driver Blues," one of the first truck driving songs. "Have I Told You Lately That I Love You" was written by Scotty Wiseman of Lulu Belle and Scotty, stars of the National Barn Dance, broadcast from WLS in Chicago during the 1930s and 1940s. Wiseman, who wrote "Remember Me (When the Candle Lights are Gleaming)" and co-wrote "Mountain Dew," wrote the song in 1944 while he was a patient at Wesley Memorial Hospital in Chicago. His wife Lulu Belle came to visit and just before she left, he said, "Have I told you lately that I love you?"

"As I lay there thinking tender thoughts about her," remembered Wiseman, "it occurred to me that this would be a good title for a song. I got paper and pencil and wrote the first verse and chorus down that afternoon." [1]. The next day, Lulu Belle came to visit and he sang it to her; she thought it was good and a

THE BEATLES AND COUNTRY MUSIC

friend of Wiseman's took it to Gene Autry in Hollywood, who was the first to record the song.

Ringo recorded an uptempo big band version of "Have I Told You Lately That I Love You," arranged by Elmer Bernstein, who won an Academy Award in 1967 for his score for *Thoroughly Modern Millie* starring Julie Andrews. Bernstein also wrote the score for the western *The Magnificent Seven* (1970), and that theme was used for years in Marlboro cigarette commercials. Bernstein also wrote the score for the western, *The Hallelujah Trail* as well as *The Ten Commandments* (1956), *To Kill a Mockingbird* (1962) and *The Great Escape* (1963).

The Beatles and Bob Dylan

In January, 1964, before their American debut on "The Ed Sullivan Show," Paul McCartney purchased Bob Dylan's *Freewheelin'* album in London. When the Beatles arrived at the George V Hotel in Paris for a three week stay, they immediately put it on the turntable in their hotel room and played it constantly. The folk album contained "Blowin' in the Wind," "Don't' Think Twice, It's All Right," "Masters of War" and "A Hard Rain's A-Gonna Fall." George Harrison said the album was "one of the most memorable things of the trip." [1]

Dylan had an immediate influence on the Beatles' songwriting. Before they left Paris, Lennon began "I'm a Loser" as he began to turn inward with his writing, projecting his own feelings. The group met Dylan in August, 1964 in New York during their American tour. At this meeting, Dylan rolled a joint and The Beatles began their life-long experience with marijuana. They had smoked it before, in Liverpool and Hamburg, but this was the first time it became a regular stimulant. The Beatles and Dylan kept up with each other and visited when they were in the same town.

Dylan in Nashville

Bob Dylan had a long association with country music, often citing Hank Williams as a major influence. In October, 1967 Dylan came to Nashville where producer Bob Johnston, head of Columbia's Nashville division, invited him to record songs for his *Blonde on Blonde* album in Columbia Studio A on Music Row. Dylan had only recorded one song for the album, "One of Us Must Know (Sooner or Later)" in New York.

Johnston brought Al Kooper and Robbie Robertson to Nashville and hired studio musicians Wayne Moss (guitar), Charlie McCoy (harmonica and trumpet), Joe South (bass) and Kenny Buttrey (drums) for the sessions that began on February 14, 1966. This is about the same time that Kris Kristofferson became the "set up" man at Columbia, although he generally referred to himself as a "janitor." A set-up man gets the studio in order, sets up the mic stands, chairs and whatever else is needed for the session, runs errands for the producer and engineer, then cleans up the studio after the musicians leave.

During the sessions held February 14-17 Dylan recorded "Visions of Johanna," "4th Time Around," "Sad Eyed Lady of the Lowlands" and "Stuck Inside of Mobile with the Memphis Blues Again." Dylan then did some concerts before he returned to Nashville for sessions March 8-10. On those sessions he recorded "Absolutely Sweet Marie," "Just Like a Woman," "Pledging My

Time," "Most Likely You'll Go Your Way (And I'll Go Mine)," "Temporary Like Achilles," "Rainy Day Women #12 & 35," "Obviously 5 Believers," "Leopard Skin Pill Box Hat" and "I Want You." Two songs, "Rainy Day Women #12 & 35" (better known as "Everybody Must Get Stoned") and "I Want You" were released as singles.

After *Blonde on Blonde,* Dylan had an accident on his motorcycle and retreated to his home in Woodstock, New York, where he recorded the songs that were later released on *The Basement Tapes.* By Fall, 1967, Dylan headed back to Nashville to record his *John Wesley Harding* album.

Dylan recorded the sparse album, playing guitar, harmonica and piano himself, supplemented by Nashville musicians Kenny Buttrey on drums and Charlie McCoy on bass, during the first two sessions. On October 17, he recorded "I Dreamed I Saw St. Augustine," "Drifter's Escape," and "The Ballad of Frankie Lee and Judas Priest." On November 6 he recorded "All Along the Watchtower," "John Wesley Harding," "As I Went Out One Morning," "I Pity the Poor Immigrant" and "I Am a Lonesome Hobo."

Johnston suggested adding a steel guitar and Dylan agreed so Johnston contacted Tommy Hill, who recommended his business partner, Pete Drake. On the final session, held November 29, Drake played steel guitar on "I'll Be Your Baby Tonight" and "Down Along the Cove." The sessions were engineered by Charlie Bragg and the album was released two days after Christmas.

In February, 1969, Dylan returned to Nashville and recorded his *Nashville Skyline* album. On that album, Johnston assembled a group of Nashville sidemen. In addition to Pete Drake, Kenny Buttrey and Charlie McCoy, who were on the *John Wesley Harding* album, musicians Norman Blake (guitar, dobro), Fred Carter, Jr. (guitar), and Bob Wilson (organ, piano) were added. During their sessions, Johnny Cash and his band, Marshall Grant (bass), W.S. Holland (drums) and Bob Wootton (electric guitar) came by and recorded a number of songs with "Girl From the North Country" included on the *Nashville Skyline* album as a duet between Cash and Dylan.

Songs on the *Nashville Skyline* album, in addition to "Girl From the North Country," are "Nashville Skyline Rag," "To Be Alone With You," "I Threw It All Away," "Peggy Day," "Lay Lady Lay," (Drummer Kenny Buttrey played bongos and cowbell on "Lay Lady Lay," which were held by set-up man/janitor Kris Kristofferson) "One More Night," "Tell Me That It Isn't True," "Country Pie" and "Tonight I'll Be Staying Here With You." This was a country album and Dylan did a guest appearance on Johnny Cash's television show to promote it.

During the period from April, 1969 to the end of March, 1970, Dylan was in Nashville several times, recording songs that are on his *Self Portrait* album. Nashville musicians on the double album once again included Pete Drake on steel guitar, Norman Blake, Kenny Buttrey, Fred Carter, Jr., Charlie Daniels, Doug Kershaw, Charlie McCoy, Bob Moore, Bill Pursell, and Bob Wilson as well as string and horn players.

The *Self Portrait* album, which included several traditional songs and songs not written by Dylan, was released in June, 1970. By that time, Dylan had begun working on his *New Morning* album, which was recorded in New York. The musicians on that album were New York session players but producer Bob Johnston, at the behest of Dylan, invited Nashville musician Charlie Daniels to New York to work on the album.

Charlie Daniels became involved with the Dylan sessions because of a comment Wayne Moss made during a session. Dylan had told the musicians on a previous session that he needed time to work on lyrics and was gone for 12 hours. (Dylan carried a typewriter with him and wrote and re-wrote lyrics.) On the next session he told the musicians he needed more time for lyrics and Wayne said "Here we go again." Dylan overheard that and told producer Bob Johnston to find another guitar player.

Charlie Daniels was a struggling musician and wanted desperately to play on a Dylan session. Johnston had Daniels sit in that session and told Dylan he'd find another guitar player for the next session but Dylan replied that he liked Daniels and wanted to keep him. According to Daniels, that decision "validated" him as a musician. After the *Self-Portrait* sessions, Dylan asked Daniels if he'd like to go to New York; Daniels agreed. [1] Daniels and Johnston were going to go to England to back Leonard Cohen on tour. Daniels was in his hotel room when Johnston called and asked if he'd like to come play bass for a jam session with Dylan and George Harrison.

On May 1, 1970, Dylan, drummer Russ Kunkel and Charlie Daniels (playing bass) were joined by Beatle George Harrison for a session that included "Working On a Guru," "Time Passes Slowly" and "If Not For You." The session could not be released because Harrison did not have a work permit; that's why the session was recorded but did not come out on an album.

Daniels stated that "George Harrison was a really nice, down-to-earth little guy, the furthest thing from what you'd think of as one of the most popular musicians in the world. He and Dylan just wanted to spend time and jam. We were standing there listening to a playback and George asked who plays steel guitar on Dylan's stuff. I said 'Pete Drake.'" Harrison wrote down his phone number and asked Daniels to give it to Pete and ask him to call. [2,3]

Harrison wanted to hire Drake for the *All Things Must Pass* sessions in England but Dylan told Harrison that Drake was a booked-up session player and probably couldn't get away for sessions outside of Nashville. Harrison decided to try anyway.

Pete Drake

Pete Drake was born in Atlanta, Georgia and, with his brothers Jack and Bill, formed The Drake Brothers. Jack and Bill Drake moved to Nashville and in 1950 Pete, then 18, came to visit. That's when he heard Jerry Byrd play steel guitar on the Grand Ole Opry and fell in love with the sound of that instrument. Back in Atlanta, Pete bought a steel guitar for $38 in a pawnshop and learned to play. He formed a group, Sons of the South in Atlanta, which included Jerry Reed, Doug Kershaw, Roger Miller, Jack Greene and Joe South; they performed on WLWA in Atlanta and WTJH in East Point, Georgia.

Pete was in the road band of Wilma Lee and Stoney Cooper and moved with them to Nashville in 1959. Drake also played in Don Gibson's and Marty Robbins' road bands and his first recording sessions were with Roy Drusky and George Hamilton IV; Drake played on Drusky's hit, "Anymore" and Hamilton's "Before This Day Ends."

The Talk Box

Alvino Rey was a pioneer in developing electric pick-ups for musical instruments; he designed the pick-up that Gibson used on their ES-150, the first commercially successful electric guitar. In 1939 Rey, a guitarist who later converted to steel guitar, worked on a "talk box." The instrument, originally called a Voder and then a Vocorder, was designed to scramble messages military leaders and field commanders sent during World War II. This instrument later became known as a Sonovox.

Rey married Luise King and later led a band which featured Luise and her sisters as vocalists, which led to their 1965 television show, "The King Family Show."

Pete Drake adapted the "talk box" to produce a "talking steel guitar," which had a plastic tube that Drake put in his mouth and sang the lyrics while he played on the steel, which was amplified. He had the idea after watching deaf neighbors communicate, then he saw a Kay Keyser movie where Alvino Rey played with a "talk box."

In 1964, he recorded a talking steel guitar song, "Forever" for Smash Records which reportedly sold over a million copies and reached number 22 on the country chart. This led to Drake's album, *Forever* and a follow-up, *Talking Steel Guitar*. Other albums followed featuring the talking steel; this led to him recording his "talking steel" on a number of country artist's recordings, beginning with "Lock, Stock and Teardrops" by Roger Miller.

Pete Drake became one of the top session musicians in Nashville, playing on numerous records; he expanded, forming a publishing company and a label, Stop Records. Among the country hits that Drake played on were "Rose Garden" by Lynn Anderson, "Behind Closed Doors" by Charlie Rich," and "Stand By Your Man" by Tammy Wynette.

George Harrison and Pete Drake

When George Harrison called Pete Drake's office, located on 18th Avenue South, just off Music Row, Drake's assistant and future wife, Rose, answered. She told Pete that George Harrison was on the line and Pete replied, "Where's he from?"

"England."

"What company is he with?"

"The Beatles."

"Let me talk to him."

"It never crossed his mind that THE George Harrison would be calling," remembered Rose. [1] The two talked and Drake told Harrison that he was booked several months ahead. Harrison replied that he'd wait and arrangements were made for Drake to travel to London to record with Harrison on his first solo project.

Pete Drake took his steel guitar, a dobro, a Harptone guitar and his "voice activator" box with him to London; accompanying him was songwriter Chuck Howard, who was signed to Pete's publishing company, Window Music. The Harptone guitar was a gift for Harrison.

At the London airport, Drake and Howard were picked up by someone driving Ringo's Rolls Royce. The car had a number of country music tapes in it, including those by Ernest Tubb and Buck Owens. When they arrived at the studio, Ringo asked, "Were you surprised that I'm really a country music fan?"

In May, 1970, George Harrison began work on his album, *All Things Must Pass*. Ringo played drums on the album; other musicians were Bobby Whitlock, Jim Gordon, Carl Radle, Bobby Keys, Jim Price, Eric Clapton, Peter Frampton, Billy Preston, Klaus Voormann, Gary Wright, Alan White and Dave Mason in addition to Drake.

Drake played on the songs "All Things Must Pass," "The Ballad of Sir Frankie Crisp," and a country song, "Behind That Locked Door."

The *All Things Must Pass* album was produced by Harrison and Phil Spector, the legendary producer known for his "Wall of Sound." On the song, "All Things Must Pass," Spector allowed the track to breathe and did not overload it with instruments playing the same thing. This allowed Drake's steel guitar to shine through.

"The Ballad of Sir Frankie Crisp" was a song about Harrison's home, Friar's Park, located in Henley-on-Thames, that was once owned by Sir Frankie Crisp (1843-1919). Crisp was an English lawyer, microscopist (he was a member of the Royal Microscopical Society) and horticulturist who developed unique gardens in his Friar's Park Estate. After Crisp's death, the estate passed to nuns, who used it as a school. It was in a state of disrepair when, in January, 1970, Harrison purchased and restored it. Pete Drake's steel guitar is prominent in the song; it is easy to hear it swimming through the recording.

Harrison had co-written songs with Dylan, including "I'd Have You Anytime," and Harrison had visited Dylan at his home in Bearsville, New York. Before Dylan's appearance on the Isle of Wight Festival at the end of August, 1969, Harrison and his wife, Patti, stayed with Dylan and his family for a week at a sixteenth-century farmhouse, Forelands Farm, near Bembridge; it had a barn, swimming pool and guards to keep fans away. Dylan's *Nashville Skyline* album had been released just prior to the Isle of Wight appearance and Dylan performed "I Threw It All Away," "I'll Be Your Baby Tonight," and "Lay Lady, Lay," all recorded in Nashville and all with a country "feel." [2] Dylan had probably brought his *Nashville Skyline* album along and Harrison heard it before the concert. As Harrison watched Dylan perform he was inspired to write "Behind That Locked Door" as an encouragement for Dylan to end his depression and seclusion and get back into the musical world. It is by far the most "country" song George Harrison ever wrote or recorded, inspired, no doubt, by Dylan's Nashville recordings.

Pete Drake and Ringo

At the Abbey Road studio, Drake and Ringo struck up a conversation and Ringo told Drake he wanted to do a country album, but wanted it done in London because albums took weeks and months to record. Drake replied that it wasn't done that way in Nashville, that Dylan only took a few days to record his albums, and that a country album for Ringo could be organized and done in a few days. Harrison and Starr had discussed Dylan and Dylan told Harrison about the speed and talent of Nashville session musicians. Drake and Starr agreed that Drake would arrange everything for him—gather songs, set up the session and produce the album.

The idea came together so quickly that there was no paperwork done with Apple Records—nothing in writing. But Pete had that

Nashville attitude of trust that things would work out and went ahead with the project. Drake believed the Ringo sessions would not only be good for him but also good for Nashville and country music, so he forged ahead.

Starr had discussed doing a country album with Bob Johnston, Dylan's producer, but Johnston wanted a lot of money to do it, so Starr dropped the idea. He briefly contemplated flying Nashville musicians to London, but finally relented to Drake's idea.

When Drake left London to return to Nashville, he left his "voice activator" box at the studio. Peter Frampton, who also played on the *All Things Must Pass* sessions, took it and the effects are heard on his hit singles, "Baby I Love Your Way," "Show Me The Way" and "Do You Feel Like I Do" on his *Frampton Comes Alive* album, which sold 11 million copies after it was released in January, 1976.

Country Music in 1970

The year 1970 began with "Baby, Baby (I Know You're a Lady)" by David Houston at number one on the *Billboard* country chart. During June, 1970, "He Loves Me All the Way" by Tammy Wynette reached number one, replacing "Hello Darlin'" by Conway Twitty. Earlier that year there were number one songs by Tom T. Hall, Sonny James, Merle Haggard ("The Fightin' Side of Me"), Charley Pride, and Marty Robbins.

During the second half of 1970 there were number one country songs by Hank Williams Jr. with the Mike Curb Congregation, Ray Price, Jerry Lee Lewis, Johnny Cash ("Sunday Morning Coming Down") and Loretta Lynn. On television, "Hee Haw,"

"The Johnny Cash Show" and "The Glen Campbell Goodtime Hour" all presented country music weekly. On the Saturday night before Ringo arrived, "The Ray Stevens Show" (billed as "Andy Williams Presents Ray Stevens") premiered.

"The Love You Save" by The Jackson 5 was the number one record on the *Billboard* Hot 100 chart when Ringo arrived in Nashville; the previous week the number one record was "The Long and Winding Road" by the Beatles, who had a number one with "Let It Be" earlier that Spring. The Jackson 5 was the hottest group on radio with three number one's that year. In many ways, it was a mellow year for pop. The year began with "Raindrops Keep Fallin' On My Head" by B.J. Thomas at number one and during the year "Close to You" by the Carpenters, "Candida" and "Knock Three Times" by Tony Orlando and Dawn, "Bridge Over Troubled Water" by Simon & Garfunkle, "Everything is Beautiful" by Ray Stevens and "Make It With You" by Bread all reached the number one position. The year ended with "My Sweet Lord" by George Harrison—recorded during the *All Things Must Pass* sessions--in the number one slot.

Beaucoups of Blues

On Monday, June 22, 1970, after his drumming on George Harrison's sessions for *All Things Must Pass* was finished, Ringo arrived in Nashville. Ringo told Pete Drake there were two things he wanted to do in Nashville: go to the Sears, Roebuck store and to Ernest Tubb's Record Shop. At Sears, Ringo bought a number of toys and shipped them back to his children, then spent the rest of the afternoon at Ernest Tubb's Record Shop on Broadway, where he bought a number of albums by country artists. The rest of the time in Nashville they worked.

Drake had booked the Music City Recorders studio at 821 19th Avenue South, which was owned by Scotty Moore, Elvis's former guitar player. Moore also served as chief engineer. Musicians booked for the session were Elvis's former drummer D.J. Fontana, guitarists Charlie Daniels, Dave Kirby, Jerry Reed, and Jerry Shook, bassist Roy Huskey, Jr., percussionist Buddy Harman, Charlie McCoy on harmonica and organ, George Richey on piano, Shorty Lavender and Jim Buchanan on fiddles, and Ben Keith on steel guitar.

Drake had contacted the writers with his publishing company to come up with songs and Chuck Howard and Sorrells Pickard provided most of the material. Howard had gotten to know Ringo during the Harrison sessions in London and Starr liked him and felt relaxed around him. The agreement, set by Allen Klein, who was managing three of the Beatles at that time, was that all the songs recorded would be published by Startling, the publishing company owned by Ringo. Drake and Ringo spent several days listening to songs with Ringo picking out the ones he wanted to do.

Pete booked Ringo in two different hotels in Nashville; one under Ringo's name to divert fans and the news media, and the other under a fake name for privacy. Ringo actually stayed at the Ramada Inn on James Robertson Parkway, the same hotel Dylan used during his visits to Nashville.

During the recording sessions, Scotty Moore hired an off-duty policemen to monitor people coming into the studio and keep out fans and on-lookers. The policeman was given a clipboard with a list of names who were approved. On the first day of recording, Ringo showed up and was stopped by the policeman. "Name please," said the policeman. "Ringo Starr." The policeman checked the list—"Ringo, Ringo, Ringo" then said, "Don't see it. You can't come in." Fortunately, Scotty's wife, Emily, was outside as well. She told the policeman, "That's Ringo Starr. He's the reason you're here!" The cop then let him in. [1]

An article in the *Nashville Tennessean* noted that Starr "recently trimmed his shoulder-length locks a bit but added a full beard" when he landed aboard a private jet at Nashville's Municipal Airport, away from the main terminal. He did not encounter fans and the news media who had expected him to arrive on June 24. The news story noted that he planned to attend the Grand Ole Opry and that George Harrison would follow "in a few weeks" and will "make an album later in the summer" in Nashville.

In the article, Drake stated that "Ringo is pretty tired. It's a long trip. Besides, all of the material he's going to record is new to him," adding that "I imagine he'll be seen a little bit later when things ease up."

"I don't know why anyone should be surprised that Ringo wants to do a country album," continued Drake. "He's a big fan of such people as Ernest Tubb, Hank Snow and Kitty Wells. For that matter, George Harrison, who knows what he's talking about, thinks Chet Atkins is as good a guitar man as ever lived." Drake also noted that Ringo had "several country tapes for the player in his Rolls-Royce."

Drake stated that "Ringo's easy to talk to, a good artist, and he really wants to do this thing," adding that "I'm glad to see people like Ringo and George coming to Nashville. It'll help us, and I like to think we have something to offer them, too."

The article noted that Ringo will be 30 "in a few days" (his birthday is July 7) and is "married to a girl he met as a fan" and is the father of two children, Zak, 5 and Jason, 4 with his wife, Maureen, pregnant. (She gave birth to a daughter later that summer.)

Reporter Gene Wyatt of the *Tennessean* noted that Ringo "now lives in an 18-room, 12th century home on a 14-acre estate purchased from Peter Sellers." Ringo and Sellers had starred in the film *The Magic Christian,* released the previous year. Wyatt acknowledged the breakup of the Beatles, which was described as a "normal process of growing up" and quoted a London writer who stated, "all of them have families now. As with any four intelligent people, their tastes and political philosophies are developing along different lines. They have enough money. Why shouldn't they try something different?" [2]

"All the writers signed to Pete started pitching songs and we even went outside the company trying to find songs," remembered Rose Drake. "It was funny because Dave Kirby was one of the best country songwriters around at that time but Ringo didn't like his sense of humor, which was very dry, so he didn't want to hear any of his songs." Pete "thought there were a couple of songs that Ringo should record because Kirby was writing hit songs but Ringo didn't want to do them." [3]

Drake sorted through the songs, then picked out some and played then for Ringo, who decided which ones he wanted to do. On Thursday, June 25, the group went into the studio and recorded four songs in the afternoon and four songs during the evening.

The next day they did the same thing and on Saturday, June 27, they finished. On Tuesday, June 29, Ringo stopped by the Quonset Hut studio and met Tammy Wynette and producer Billy Sherrill, who were in a recording session. A picture in the newspaper noted that Starr "just dropped by to dig" the session because he was a fan. [4]

Another article by Gene Wyatt in the *Tennessean,* headlined "'Country Ringo' Breezes Through Quick Sessions," noted Ringo had recorded eight songs by midnight, June 26 and "it would have taken weeks to do that in England." The article reiterated that George Harrison had plans to come to Nashville "later in the summer" and that Ringo was scheduled to visit the Grand Ole Opry and "appear briefly on stage."

The article reported that "a modest platoon of Beatle fans, mostly female, patrolled the street outside" during the session and "there were a few sub-teen youngsters, several escorted by parents, anxious for a look at the Beatle" and that "one boy held a tiny tape machine, hoping to record for posterity any Beatle sound which might seep outside. None did."

Drake stated that "Ringo likes the material, and he's doing it well. He hasn't had time to learn it all yet and we'll be dubbing his parts in the first of next week." Drake planned to add his steel guitar later as well.

"The songs are all pure country," said Drake. "They're by some of the best writers—Sorrells Pickard, Larry Kingston, Chuck Howard did three. There are all types: hard, middle of the road, some with a stronger beat than you usually hear."

The journalist stated that Ringo "looked relaxed in a long-sleeve magenta shirt with the neck open almost to the waist, and mixed paisley and broad pin-stripe flared pants held up with a wide belt and oversize silver buckle" and that his beard "is now trimmed in Fu Manchu style." Ringo wore "a brown suede vest and sharply pointed tan shoes. There was a modified Maltese cross on a chain around his neck and heavy rings on his right index and left ring fingers. He smoked his cigarette very short, European fashion."

The reporter wrote that during the recording of "The Fifteen Dollar Draw," Drake told the musicians to "add a little gut before the Dobro starts" and that "the tempo's fine, if we can get everybody to play the same one," eliciting laughs from the studio musicians. Four takes later, Ringo and Drake came into the control room and "listened intently to the playback turned to an almost deafening level." [5]

Ringo's Songs With The Beatles

In his book, *Here, There and Everywhere,* Geoff Emerick, who engineered a number of Beatles sessions at Abbey Road, stated that Ringo was "very uptight and nervous when it came to singing, and with good reason: he knew he was no vocalist, and he had to be coached and nurtured around the mic." [1]

Most of the Beatles albums had a song where Ringo had the lead vocal, "despite the fact that he could barely sing," stated Emerick. "But the fans ate it up, and I have to admit there was something endearing about his voice—even if it was just the fact that you could hear him constantly straining to stay on pitch." Because of his limited vocal talent, Lennon and McCartney "would try to write him a song that had only a few notes in the melody line." [2] On the *Revolver* album, it was "Yellow Submarine" and on the *Sergeant Pepper* album it was "With a Little Help From My Friends." On earlier albums Ringo sang lead on "I Wanna Be Your Man," "Matchbox," "Boys" and "What Goes On." Later, Ringo sang the songs he wrote, "Don't Pass Me By" and "Octopus's Garden" then, on the *Abbey Road* album, sang Lennon's "Goodnight."

"Don't Pass Me By" is a country song that Ringo was working on when he joined the Beatles; it was recorded for the *White Album* and Hunter Davies, in his book on the Beatles lyrics, states "It's a country and western number with a mean fiddle." "Octopus's Garden," also credited to Ringo alone as the writer, was on the *Abbey Road* album and Hunter Davies states "It's a jolly, popular song, with a country and western beat." [3]

Ringo remembered that "I wrote 'Don't Pass Me By' when I was sitting around at home. I only play three chords on the guitar and three on the piano. I was fiddling with the piano—I just bang away—and then if a melody comes and some words, I just have to keep going. That's how it happened. I was just sitting at home alone and 'Don't Pass Me By' arrived. We played it with a country attitude....It was a very exciting time for me and everyone was really helpful, and recording that crazy violinist was a thrilling moment." [4]

Ringo During The Nashville Sessions

Mac Evans, who was second engineer on the Ringo sessions, was impressed with Ringo because of "just how nice" he was.

"He was just down to earth and conversational and was having an absolute ball," remembered Evans. "He was in seventh Heaven—on a cloud—because he was getting involved in the recording. This was the first time he'd been actively involved in recording his own music. With the Beatles, the other guys would cut him a track and give it to him and say 'learn to sing this.' He said that was the way it was in the past and it was just so good to have the musicians around so he could talk to them and feel what they were playing. He got into the Nashville Sound pretty quick." [1]

It is true that Ringo tended to play a secondary role, even when a song he sang lead on with the Beatles was recorded. The songs were usually composed by Lennon and McCartney, who then told Ringo that a song was "his" song. For "With a Little Help From My Friends," the backing track was recorded first, then Ringo sang the song, having a difficult time hitting the last big note. On "Good Night" on *The Beatles* (better known as *The White Album*) John Lennon, who wrote the song, was originally going to sing it but decided to let Ringo do it. The group recorded demos of the songs they recorded at George Harrison's house (the first time they had done so) and Lennon gave Ringo the demo to take home and learn. [2]

Scotty Moore stated that "to everyone's surprise, Ringo blended in exceptionally well with the other musicians. Every once in a while, they had a little fun with him…Southern boys only fun around with people they like, or people they think they might be about to like."

"He worked like a real trouper," said Scotty. "We were using head arrangements that we made up on the spot. He only had three days to learn the songs. He would start singing and all the pickers would put it together."

"Whatever we wanted to do was fine with him," said drummer D.J. Fontana. "Sure, he struggled with the vocals, but I thought he did a good job. He's not a bad singer at all. He has that little English accent." [3]

"It wasn't that quick and easy," remembered Evans. "I remember that after we did the tracks we did some overdubs. It wasn't just a single guitar player coming in to do a lick. It was three or four great guitar players playing together on the track which, to me was so unique."

"The last thing we did was the jam session and that's the only thing I engineered," said Evans. "The reason I engineered was because Scotty played on that." Ringo played drums. "I don't remember exactly how it happened, but Scotty said 'Take over, I've got to play guitar.' The whole session group played and it ran over 15 minutes or more. I ran out of multi-track tape but I had the two-track running and we had plenty of tape on that. But we were running the 16-track at 30 ips (inches per second) and it ran out of tape so we just kept on going on that two track. It was mixed pretty well from the board."

Ringo "was very well prepared and he was so high just on doing that session," said Evans. "He was just floating on the air and anything you asked him to do, he'd do double. He would come back between cuts and just stand around, having coffee with all the guys. He'd stand in the tape room and we'd talk. He was just a genuine, straight-forward nice guy. He had no airs about being a star or millionaire or anything like that. I'd love for all people who do sessions to be like him."

"He was just a whiz on country music," continued Evans. "He knew the history of country music and he knew most of the newer songs on the radio. He was right up to date and he could fit into any conversation you could have on country music." [4]

On Wednesday, July 1, Starr flew back to London. Before he left, Ringo gave Drake one of his silk shirts because Pete "had kidded him throughout the session about his wild clothes."

Songs on the original LP were "Beaucoups of Blues," written by Buzz Rabin, "Love Don't Last Long" by Chuck Howard, "Fastest Growing Heartache in the West" by Larry Kingston and Frank Dycus, "Without Her" by Sorrells Pickard, "Woman of the Night" by Pickard, "I'd Be Talking All The Time" by Chuck Howard and Larry Kingston, "$15 Draw" by Pickard, "Wine, Women and Loud Happy Songs" by Larry Kingston, "I Wouldn't Have You Any Other Way" by Chuck Howard (recorded as a duet with Jeannie Kendall), "Loser's Lounge" by Bobby Pierce, "Waiting" by Chuck Howard and "Silent Home Coming" by Pickard.

Jeannie Kendall

Jeannie Kendall and her father, Royce, were part of the duo, The Kendalls. Originally from St. Louis, where Royce and his wife had a barber shop and beauty salon, the Kendall family attended the Grand Ole Opry in the late 1960s and when they returned home decided to finance their own record. A St. Louis disc jockey brought it to the attention of Pete Drake, who signed the duo to his label, Stop Records. Their first single, "Leavin' On a Jet Plane," written by John Denver, reached number 52 on the country chart in 1970. The Kendalls were on the Stop label when Pete Drake brought Ringo to Nashville in 1970 and so he had her sing a duet with Ringo on "I Wouldn't Have It Any Other Way."

Extra Songs

Not included on the vinyl album was "Nashville Jam," which was credited to everyone who was in the studio at the time: Chuck Howard, Sorrells Pickard, Jim Buchanan, Charlie Daniels, Pete Drake, D.J. Fontana, Buddy Harman, Junior Huskey, Ben Keith, Dave Kirby, Charlie McCoy, Jerry Reed, George Richey and Jerry Shook. The final song, "The Wishing Book" was never released.

Marshall Fallwell Photographer

Marshall Fallwell was a graduate student at Vanderbilt University, working on his Ph.D. in English; his dissertation was an English translation of a fifteenth century manuscript, *The Art of War*. Marshall's wife had gotten him into photography but he was not a professional photographer until the writer from *Rolling Stone* magazine asked him to take pictures for a story about Ringo in Nashville.

Pete Drake knew about Marshall because a month before the Ringo sessions Fallwell had taken pictures of Tracy Nelson and Mother Earth for their album that Pete produced at Scotty Moore's studio. When Pete said he needed pictures for the Ringo session "I jumped in," said Marshall. He borrowed a camera from a friend at Vanderbilt; his wife had a box camera "but I wanted a Nikon" for that assignment.

After taking pictures inside the studio during the session, Marshall was leaving the studio to take the borrowed camera back when Neil Aspinall, the Beatles former road manager who was then working for Apple Records, stopped and asked if he could take a picture for the album cover. "They wanted a blue tinged photo for the cover," remembered Fallwell. "That was easy to do, you just take indoor film and shoot it outdoors. Neil also said that all pictures taken for that assignment belonged to Apple and he gave me, I think, $600."

"Ringo was an extremely nice fellow," said Fallwell. "He pulled me aside and asked 'Where can we go?' for the album cover shot. I said 'We'll go to Tracy Nelson's place' and he said 'Who's that?' We were in the studio so Scotty played 'Careless Love' by Tracy and he liked that. So we went out to Tracy's farm in Mt. Juliet, about 30 miles east of Nashville. There was an old log building where they used to keep hams and that's where we took the picture."

Later, Marshall drove Ringo around Nashville because "he wanted to see the town," said Fallwell. "In Hillsboro Village there was a Sgt. Pepper's Head Shop with bongs and tie-dyed t-shirts. Ringo said, 'Stop! I've got to go in there.' There were a lot of people in there so he asked, 'Do we need to be careful?' and I said, 'No—not in Nashville. Nobody is going to grab you.' It was really crowded. Ringo walked around a rack of clothes and bumped into a 16 or 17 year old girl. She turned around and said, 'OH MY GOD—IT'S HIM!' Everybody knew he was in town because it had been in the newspapers. Ringo stopped and talked to this girl. Before long everyone on the street knew and there was a big crowd but they were very polite. A lot of people wanted to touch him as we worked our way back to the car." [1]

George's Note to Pete

On July 7, 1970, George Harrison's mother, Louise, died in Liverpool; she was 58. In a hand-written letter dated July 12 from Friar Park, Harrison wrote to Pete Drake.

Dear Pete,

Thank you for the 'Harptone' it really is a great guitar and the nicest sounding acoustic I've heard. I've been busy lately in the North of England and haven't heard Ringo's album as yet, but from the people who have, they tell me it is really good and you did a good job on it. Whatever happens I feel some goodwill must be created between Country and Popular music people after what we've been doing with you lately. I certainly hope they all like it out there. Thanks also for the amplifier, I can't wait to get back in the studio and use it properly.

Well, love to all you Hillbilly Folk out there from us all here in England and I'll be seeing you sometime in the future. Give my best to Chuck and thank you again Pete for the Instruments.

Best wishes

George Harrison (1)

My Sweet Lord is So Fine

George Harrison's "My Sweet Lord" was a huge hit in 1970. He had written the song based on the Chiffon's "He's So Fine." In a court case brought by the publisher of "He's So Fine," Harrison argued the infringement was accidental, although the court found him guilty of a violation of copyright.

"He's So Fine" had been sung amongst the musicians in the studio during the time Harrison recorded "My Sweet Lord." Apparently, this led Pete Drake to produce "He's So Fine" on country singer Jody Miller after he returned from England. The record was released in 1971 and became a top five country hit for Miller.

George and Nashville

Despite his interest in Nashville and country music as well as his admiration for Chet Atkins, George Harrison never made it to Nashville.

The simple answer is that he was doing other things. In 1971, the year after *All Things Must Pass,* Harrison spent a great deal of time working on the benefit Concert for Bangla Desh, held at Madison Square Garden. The concert was held in August, then the film came out the next year. This was followed by a series of albums from Harrison.

When Harrison came to the United States it was usually to Los Angeles or New York; when he traveled to places other than the United States it was usually India.

If George Harrison had come to Nashville to record it would have been a media circus and Harrison detested the trappings of stardom. There was no compelling reason for him to come to Nashville and the singer was world weary of being a celebrity so, although he had an early interest in Nashville, his post- Beatles career did not lead him in that direction.

Norbert Putnam and David Briggs

On February 11, 1964—two days after the Beatles appeared on the Ed Sullivan Show, they played their first concert in America in Washington, D.C. at the Sports Arena. The Beatles had toured with Tommy Roe in England during 1963 and asked him to open for them in Washington. Knowing that Roe recorded in Muscle Shoals, they asked if he would bring the Muscle Shoals Rhythm Section as a backing band.

In Muscle Shoals, Rick Hall opened a studio, FAME (Florence Alabama Music Enterprises) in 1960 after a career that included playing in an Army band that featured Faron Young and Gordon Terry, then played with a country group, Carmol Taylor and the Country Pals. He teamed with Billy Sherrill (who later produced George Jones, Tammy Wynette, and David Houston and was co-writer on "Stand By Your Man," "Almost Persuaded," "Too Far Gone," "I Don't Wanna Play House," and numerous other songs as head of CBS's country division in Nashville) and the two wrote songs. Hall had initial success writing songs for George Jones ("Aching Breaking Heart"), Brenda Lee ("She'll Never Know") and Roy Orbison ("Sweet and Innocent").

At the FAME studio Hall recruited musicians from local bands to form the original Muscle Shoals Rhythm Section, which was comprised of Norbert Putnam (bass), David Briggs (keyboards), Jerry Carrigan (drums) and Terry Thompson (guitar). The first hit from Muscle Shoals was "You Better Move On" by Arthur Alexander. The Beatles loved Arthur Alexander and recorded one of Alexander's songs, "Anna," on their first British album. Tommy Roe's first hit, "Sheila," was recorded with the Muscle Shoals Rhythm Section and the Beatles recorded that song on a BBC "Light Programme" show, "Here We Go" in October, 1962.

Tommy Roe and Chris Montez were on a theatre package tour with The Beatles beginning March 9, 1963 and ending March 31. During this tour, John Lennon missed several dates from sickness; the songs the Beatles did on this tour were "Love Me Do," "Misery," "A Taste of Honey," "Do You Want To Know a Secret," "Please Please Me" and "I Saw Her Standing There."

Roe came back to the FAME studio enthused about the Beatles with a rough demo tape of the group with McCartney playing guitar and John and George singing harmony. "The first thing we egotistical studio musicians noticed was the B string on the guitar was flat," remembered Putnam. "We looked at each other like 'They may be great but they can't tune a guitar" and "it was the most trite lyric. Something about 'I want to hold your hand,' and the chord progression was a stock Isley Brothers chord progression that had been used in a million songs." When John and George joined in on harmony "it was so out of tune that Rick Hall stopped the tape machine and said something like 'Tommy, I don't know what you've been smoking, but these guys can't play or sing.'"

"It was the worst demo you've ever heard," remembered Putnam. "That was pretty damn bad [but] George Martin took those boys to school. I think George Martin kicked them up three or four notches pretty fast."

Tommy Roe insisted the Beatles were a great talent, telling his producer, Felton Jarvis, that when the Beatles played "the crowd went berserk" and "I could hardly follow them on stage." Tommy told the musicians "They've got something." "I think Tommy might have been the only one to know that," said Putnam. [1]

The Muscle Shoals Rhythm Section flew to Washington and landed in a snowstorm around 3 p.m. and went straight to the Sports Arena, which seated about 8,000 and was not set up as a concert arena; it was usually the scene of boxing matches. The musicians carried their instruments in and did a quick sound check, more excited about backing up the Righteous Brothers than appearing on a show with the Beatles, according to David Briggs and Norbert Putnam. (A poster of that concert shows The Caravelles, Tommy Roe and The Chiffons as opening acts.)

After sound check, the musicians had dinner—missing the Beatles sound check--and when they returned found an invitation to attend a reception for the Beatles at the British Embassy at midnight. The musicians were scheduled to leave on an 11:30 flight back to Nashville that night and decided to tear up the invitations and throw them in the trash.

Tommy Roe did two songs that night, "Sheila" and "Everybody"—which was his current hit, and the musicians were upset "with all those teenagers" because they were "yelling and screaming and they're not listening to the Righteous Brothers," said Putnam.

As the Beatles went on stage a police escort came for the Alabama musicians but they decided to stay, armed with new 8 mm cameras. "We didn't have that much film," remembered Putnam, "so I'd shoot eight or ten seconds and then I'd stop."

The Beatles started their concert with George singing "Roll Over Beethoven," then followed with "From Me To You," "I Saw Her Standing There," "This Boy," "All My Loving," "I Wanna Be Your Man," "Please Please Me," "Til There Was You," "She Loves You," "I Want To Hold Your Hand," "Twist and Shout" and finished with "Long Tall Sally."

The Muscle Shoals musicians were blown away because "We'd never heard a band that loud. And it's coming off their amps because it's not in the sound system, which is above their heads. My God those amps were loud, and the guitars were loud," remembered Putnam. "We were up there playing with our American Fender amplifiers. I had a Fender bass with fourteen inch speakers and a bass reflex cabinet on the back of it, which probably doubled its output. Terry Thompson was playing through a Fender Twin. David Briggs played a Wurlitzer electric piano and that was the only keyboard. Jerry Carrigan was playing drums and there was no amplification for the rhythm section. Only the voices of the singers were in the P.A. The Beatles came out with these Super Vox amplifiers (60 watts). The sound level that came off the stage was about double the sound level we had just played at. It was an order of magnitude of at least three or four times and it was exciting! They were the first really loud rock band." [2]

Prior to the concert the Beatles had said they loved "jelly babies," which were soft candies in England but hard "jelly beans" in America and during the concert the Beatles were pelted with those hard candies. It was the first time the Beatles had performed "in the round" and they stood on the boxing ring, whose ropes had been taken down, and performed a few songs, then shifted their equipment around (Ringo had to shuffle his drum set around) then performed a few more songs before shifting around again so at any one time the Beatles had their backs to three fourths of the audience.

The Alabama musicians decided they might like to go to the reception at the British Embassy but when they went back to the trash cans where they had discarded their invitations, the trash had been emptied. The scene at the British Embassy was crowded with teenagers and someone sniped a lock from Ringo's hair, which caused the Beatles to make a quick exit. Back at the Shoreham Hotel, Tommy Roe drank a beer while the press scrambled for interviews and quotes in a chaotic crowd.

Norbert Putnam, David Briggs, Jerry Carrigan and Terry Thompson caught their 11:30 flight back to Nashville, then drove for two hours to Muscle Shoals and the next day did a recording session. They carried with them their 8 mm film (with no sound) and memories of their first glimpse of Beatlemania.

A few years later, Putnam, Briggs and Carrigan moved to Nashville (Terry Thompson died in 1965) where they became ace studio musicians and played on a number of hits by country artists, including those by Elvis at RCA Studio B.

Marshall Fallwell: Rock Photographer

After those photos of Ringo came out credited to Marshall Fallwell, "My phone didn't stop ringing for a number of years," he said. In 1971 Fallwell went to France and took pictures of the Rolling Stones during their *Exile on Main Street* sessions. He remained a popular photographer until 1985 when "I decided I never wanted to take another picture of a guy with a guitar again." [1]

America in 1970

During the time that Ringo was in a Nashville studio recording, James Brown was also recording in a Nashville studio at Starday on Dickerson Road while Chet Atkins was performing in concert in Boston with the Boston Pops. In the news was the pullout from Cambodia as the Vietnam war raged on. An article by George Gallup in the *Nashville Banner* stated that "56 percent of people believe we made a mistake sending troops to fight in Vietnam" and "citizens who think we were wrong to commit our forces to Vietnam has more than doubled over the last five years." [1] Demonstrations by students protesting the Vietnam War were on numerous college campuses.

A survey by Gallup listed "campus unrest as the nation's number one problem," ahead of the Vietnam war, racial strife, the high cost of living and crime." Columnist Clayton Fritchey quoted a poll "which found that college demonstrators were more hated than prostitutes, athiests, and homosexuals." The columnist noted that "there is no doubt that the students have generated an unreasoning fury on the part of their elders." [2]

The Beatles, the most popular musical group for American youth, were held responsible by many conservative Americans for most of the problems created by young long-haired "hippies." Many, if not most, Americans classified all young people with long hair and jeans as "hippies," although the actual hippies were a small percentage of young people. Still, it was all in one big pot according to those Americans who viewed young men with long hair as anti-American, even Communists. It was not unusual for a long-haired young man to be confronted by conservative short-haired young men who wanted to beat them up or made snide comments like "I thought you were a girl."

On July 4, just after Ringo left Nashville, there were two events held that highlighted this generation gap. In Washington an "Honor America" day was held on the country's 194th birthday. Reverend Billy Graham as the main speaker and he gave a conciliatory, uplifting speech before an estimated crowed of 35,000 on the Washington Mall. Graham told the audience that "We will listen respectfully to those who dissent in accordance with the constitutional principles, but we strongly reject violence and the erosion of any of our liberties under the guise of a dissent that promises everything and delivers only chaos."

At the Washington rally, according to newspaper reports, "about 300 persons in hippie garb chanted obscenities through some of the prayers" during the inter-faith service and "splashed around noisily in the reflecting pool...and clashed with police." [3]

Young men and young women all over America protested the Vietnam War and the draft; even though they were sent to fight, they were too young to vote. They had a direct stake in this conflict: They were required to fight—and possibly die—in a war they believed was wrong. In Boston, the right wing John Birch Society held a pro-war rally.

In Byron, Georgia, the "Second Annual Atlanta International Pop Festival" attracted 500,000 for a three day festival that featured The Allman Brothers, The Radars, Grand Funk Railroad, John Sebastian, Ten Years After and Cat Mother and the All-Night News Boys in an outdoor concert where temperatures passed the 100 degree mark. Georgia Governor Lester Maddox, who began his political career by vowing to never serve Negros in his fried chicken restaurant, called the festival "a shame and disgrace… and something to be expected among savages." The festival, held about 90 miles south of Atlanta, was "the worst thing that ever happened in this area of the country," said Byron Mayor Ed Green. "I don't know if we will ever recover."

According to newspaper reporters, there were "tales of nude swimming, naked strollers, open fornication and widespread drug use during the festival." The Mayor stated he "would take legal steps—and possibly appeal to the legislature—to prevent the festival's return next year." [4]

Hair

When the Beatles first appeared on "The Ed Sullivan Show," the chief topic the following day was not their music but their hair. When the Beatles arrived, America was a crew-cut nation with short hair the accepted norm. During the ensuing years, young men let their hair grow long and this angered many older Americans who saw long hair as a threat, a symbol of dope inhaling hippies bent on destroying America. Those who protested the Vietnam War—generally college students—were labeled Communists and worse. Long hair was a signifier during the 1960s and early 1970s and for many it signified an anti-American attitude and dangerous radicalism that threatened the core values of America.

Paul McCartney, looking back at their first appearance on "The Ed Sullivan Show" stated, "We came out of nowhere with funny hair, looking like marionettes or something. That was very influential. I think that was really one of the big things that broke us—the hairdo more than the music, originally. A lot of people's fathers had wanted to turn us off. They told their kids, 'Don't be fooled, they're wearing wigs.'" [1]

Preachers regularly denounced young men wearing long hair, citing 1 Corinthians 11:14 from the Bible, which states, "Does not even nature itself teach you that if a man has long hair it is a disgrace to him, but that if a woman has long hair, it is her glory?" According to those preachers as well as conservative Americans, men who had long hair were a disgrace, sissies and perhaps even homosexuals and Communists.

In a column by William Buckley in the *Nashville Banner,* titled "Long Hair: A Symbol of the Exhibitionist," the columnist noted he recently read an article, 'Why Hair Has Become a Four-letter Word' which discussed the long-hair-short hair debate through the ages and stated (after quoting the biblical verse in 1 Corinthians) "it was generally thought by the authorities over the years that men with beards are men to be feared, and it is interesting that Fidel Castro, who did more than anybody in the modern age to identify long hair and radicalism, came quietly to realize the same conclusion when in 1968 he banned longhair at Havana University."

Buckley stated that his "own tendency in these matters is permissive" but wondered "why it is that a spirit of something half way between disgust and anger wells up within me at true excessiveness...particularly among teenagers. I think I know the reason, and it has nothing to do with sex or revolution. It has to do with exhibitionism." [2]

In a Letter to the Editor in the *Nashville Banner* on July 4, 1970, a young man wrote that he had opened the door of a hardware store to help "a real old man" with a cane who, after he went through the door, turned to the young long-haired man and "just stood there and looked at me. The first thing he said was, 'There's nothing like having a girl hold the door for you.'" This angered the young man who said, "I don't think I'll ever hold the door for any old man again. How can I be expected to have respect for him, if he has none for me?" [3]

An article titled "About That Rug on Your Neck, Pal" by AP reporter Richard Blystone stated that young men with longhair were disqualified from receiving unemployment checks in Monterey, California, "under a ruling that too much hair restricts availability for jobs." In Detroit, two young "dissidents" took a sheriff to court after he ordered their heads shaved in the county jail. The writer looked at historical figures and their length of hair, then noted, "the wrong type of growth on the other fellow's head has been like fingernails on the blackboard to generations of men."

Many Americans believed that having long hair meant a young man was politically "liberal" or even "radical" but the article quoted a study by an anthropologist from the University of Dayton who concluded that "one can accurately guess a youth's radicalism by his hair style only about 54% of the time."

The writer then quoted an author who postulated why long hair was so controversial. One reason was that the over 30 age group is "jealous" because they've lost their hair. Another reason was that the body language of long haired young men said to the older generation "We don't want to grow up the way you are. We don't want to work in the tower you've created. This disturbs us. To an older guy it says they're rejecting our values and therefore we're not good." A third reason was that "longhair to [the columnist's] generation is equated with femininity" and that "longhair looks like a threat to those of us who are a little unsure of their masculinity and this explains why such a little thing can arouse such a violent reaction." [4]

During the time when long-hair on young men was viewed as a signifier of radical political beliefs, a fist shaking at conservative values, and an effort to undermine middle class society, the Beatles kept growing their hair longer and longer.

The stereotypes were not all on one side. Many young men with long hair who were accosted for their looks considered all politically conservative Americans to be racists, bigots, hypocrites and rednecks. Many of those conservative Americans loved country music, which became part of the counter to the counterculture. In 1969 Merle Haggard recorded "Okie From Muskogee," an anthem for country fans who did not "let their hair grow long and shaggy like the hippies out in San Francisco do." This was the song that articulated the thoughts and feelings of the "silent majority." The following year, Haggard had a number one country record with "Fightin' Side of Me," whose lyrics state he's "heard people talkin' bad about the way we have to live here in this country" with the final line "when you're running down our country, hoss, you're walking on the fightin' side of me." Bumper stickers proclaimed "America—Love it or Leave it" and there was a huge gap that grew between generations. To the older, conservative crowd, young men who wore long hair loved rock music, hated America and were unmanly while country music fans wore short hair, bathed regularly and were good, decent, God-fearing true Americans.

Ringo and Country Music

Ringo did not fit the mold of what a country artist should look like or think like at that time so, consequently, he was never accepted as a "country" artist; instead, he was viewed as a rock artist who made a country album. The end result was that Ringo Starr's country songs were not played much on country radio or accepted by the country audience, although *Beaucoups of Blues* reached number 35 on *Billboard's* country album chart.

The rock audience didn't particularly care for the album, either. It did chart on the *Billboard* pop chart (#65) and the single reached number 85, but sales were not as strong as expected for a former Beatle. This was during a period when there was a huge divide between the worlds of country and rock. Country music represented a conservative America, the "silent majority" and the people Merle Haggard sang about in "Okie From Muskogee." Rock, according to the traditional country audience, represented the counterculture of free love, smoking grass, LSD, hippies, long hair in a short hair world, and unwashed masses high on drugs.

Ringo, for his part, loved country music and probably felt that his album would be accepted by the country audience. After all, he was a Beatle—a group with a huge following—and the album was definitely, in terms of sound, Nashville Country. There were reports that Capitol, which distributed the Beatles' label Apple in the United States, never really pushed the album; it fell in the cracks with the pop promotion department unable to reach the pop audience and the country promotion staff out of the loop.

After Beaucoups of Blues

Ringo's follow-ups did much better; his next seven singles were all top ten on the *Billboard* pop chart ("Back Off Boogaloo," "Photograph," "You're Sixteen," "Oh My My," "Only You" and "No No Song") and two ("Photograph" and "You're Sixteen") reached number one on *Billboard's* Hot 100 chart. His two following albums, *Ringo* and *Goodnight Vienna*, both reached the top ten on *Billboard's* pop album chart.

The album after *Beaucoups of Blues* was *Ringo*, and "You're Sixteen" was an old Johnny Burnette song while another song on that album, "Sunshine Life For Me" featured country fiddles. Ringo did not abandon country music when he left Nashville, but he learned how to channel it into something that fit him and his fans from the Beatle days.

Ringo did not give up recording country songs; on his *Goodnight Vienna* album, released in 1974, he recorded Roger Miller's "Husbands and Wives." On his *Stop and Smell the*

Roses album (1981) Nashville steel guitarist Lloyd Green played on three songs ("Private Property," "Can't Fight Lightning" and an old Carl Perkins song, "Sure to Fall") produced by Paul McCartney; he also recorded "You Belong to Me," a song written by Country Music Hall of Famer Pee Wee King with Redd Stewart and Chilton Price. On his *I Wanna Be Santa Claus* album (1999), Ringo recorded "Blue Christmas" and on his albums *Ringo Rama* (2003), *Choose Love* (2005), *Liverpool 8* (2008) and *Y Not* (2008) he had country-ish songs.

On his album *Ringo 2012* (2012), he reached back to his early Liverpool days and recorded "Rock Island Line" and a Buddy Holly song, "Think It Over" as well as a song co-written by Gary Nicholson.

Gary Burr and Gary Nicholson

During his solo career Ringo wrote songs with songwriters Gary Burr and Gary Nicholson, who had success writing country songs.

Gary Nicholson had four songs recorded by Ringo: "Never Without You," "Peace Dream," "Wonderful" and "Satisfied." None of them are "country" songs but "Never Without You," written with Mark Hudson and Ringo, is in memory of George Harrison and has a nice, easy loping feel.

Gary Burr was a former member of Pure Prairie League, replacing Vince Gill. Burr's first hit was "Love's Been a Little Bit Hard on Me" by Juice Newton. Other country hits include "I Try to Think About Elvis" by Patti Loveless, "Burned Like a Rocket" by Billy Joe Royal, "That's My Job" by Conway Twitty, "Sure

Love" by Hal Ketchum," "What Mattered Most" by Ty Herndon and songs recorded by Garth Brooks, Reba McEntire, Faith Hill, Kenny Rogers, Ricky Van Shelton, LeAnn Rimes, Gary Allen, Chely Wright, Tim McGraw, Wynonna and Billy Ray Cyrus.

Burr has co-written a number of songs with Ringo, including "Trippin' On My Own Tears," "Tuff Love," "The Turnaround," "Think About You," "Can't Do It Wrong," "Choose Love," "Don't Hang Up," "Elizabeth Reigns," "English Garden," "Fading In, Fading Out," "Free Drinks," "Give Me Back the Beat," "Hard To Be True," "Harry's Song," "If It's Love That You Want," "Imagine Me There," "Love First, Ask Questions Later," "Love Is," "Memphis On Your Mind," "Now That She's Gone Away," "Oh My Lord," "Pasodobles," "R U Ready," "Some People," "Think About You," "What Love Wants To Be," "Write One For Me" and "Wrong All the Time."

"Ringo loves country music, but his tastes run more towards the older, traditional artists like Hank Williams," said Gary Burr. "He loves the Texas guys. Ray Wylie Hubbard is a favorite of his and he's a fan of Steve Earle. He played me some old songs from the 1920s and '30s and showed me where Hank Williams got his melodies. [1]

Gary Burr met Ringo through Mark Hudson, Ringo's producer and an old friend of Gary's. Ringo decided to resume recording and touring in the early twenty-first century and Gary was asked to join the touring band, which became "The Roundheads." They worked together 2005-2008.

During the recording of the *Choose Love* album, "It was pretty much like any songwriting session," remembered Burr, "if you put aside who it was." The album was recorded at the studio in Ringo's home outside of London. On "Give Me Back the Beat," written by Ringo, Mark Hudson, Burr, Steve Dudas and Dean Grakal, "Ringo came in around noon—I'd gotten there earlier in the morning," said Burr, "and he said 'I was on the treadmill and this was in my head,' then said 'give me back the beat' and asked, 'Anything there?'"

"It was a drummer's title," said Burr, "and Charlie Watts and Ringo were both supposed to play drums on it but the day before the recording, Charlie was diagnosed with cancer so it didn't happen. That would have been the first time that the drummers of both the Rolling Stones and Beatles played on the same song."

At the songwriting sessions, held in Ringo's studio, the writers gathered together in the morning and Ringo arrived around noon, after a workout and breakfast; Ringo was happy and in a good mood by this time. "Sometimes he'd pull out a scrap of paper with an idea he'd written down or sometimes he'd just say 'I want to write a ballad, or a reggae or something like that,'" remembered Burr. "The artist always gets the first shot of what he wants to do. If he didn't have something to start, we'd write all day, take a break for dinner—we'd go into the little village and have dinner— and then come back, lay down a track and keep going until we'd finished it. Sometimes we'd add some things in the morning."

"We'd write on whatever instrument we picked up," said Burr. "Sometimes I'd have a guitar and sometimes I'd have a bass so that's what we'd play on the track." Burr even whistled at the end of their recording of "Harry's Song."

Harry Nilsson was Ringo's best friend and, as the song progressed, "Ringo said it reminded him of Harry so we wrote in that direction," said Burr. "It's in a rootie toot sort of style." That song was on the *Liverpool 8* album.

"Write One for Me" came about because Burr and Hudson were at a songwriting conference in Miami and were headed to Ringo's house in Los Angeles, where he also had a studio, for the next project. Ringo and Hudson spoke on the phone and, as they were hanging up, Ringo said, "if you have a spare minute, write one for me." The idea clicked immediately with Burr "and Mark and I worked on that and then Ringo finished it."

During the tours, the band members usually arrived at the venue in the morning for a sound check. The band members usually ended up jamming and, since all the band members were Beatle fans, they'd often jam on Beatles songs. Sometimes they'd be jamming on a Beatles song when Ringo arrived around noon. Ringo would always say "all right, all right, that's enough" and the band would quit. However, one day they were playing "Ticket to Ride" and Ringo came in, sat on the drums, and started playing. "He couldn't remember the drums on that song at first," said Burr, "but you see him gradually remember it and he got the beat and played a bit before he said 'all right, all right, that's enough!'" [2]

Most of the songs Burr and Ringo have written would be classified as "rock" but, like many Beatle's songs, you can also hear a touch of country in there as well.

Changes in Nashville During the 1970s

By the early 1970s, things had changed quite a bit in Nashville. The Nashville Sound had broadened the appeal of country music with large orchestras backing hits by Ray Price, Eddy Arnold and

Charlie Rich, much to the chagrin of long-time country fans who came of age during the honky tonk era of Webb Pierce, Ernest Tubb and Buck Owens.

The singer-songwriter era in pop, ushered in by the likes of James Taylor, Carole King and Billy Joel saw Kris Kristofferson emerge as a major songwriter and recording artist in country music. Kristofferson wrote "For the Good Times" for Ray Price, "Help Me Make It Through the Night" for Sammi Smith, "Sunday Morning Coming Down" for Johnny Cash and "Me and Bobby McGee," first recorded by Roger Miller and then a rock hit by Janis Joplin. He grew his hair long and was embraced by the rock world.

In 1974 there were hits on country radio by former R&B singers Charlie Rich and Ronnie Milsap and that year Rich won the Country Music Association's "Entertainer of the Year" while pop artist Olivia Newton-John was voted the Country Music Association's "Female Vocalist." Waylon Jennings with his heavy rock beat on drums and guitar had his first number one hits with "This Time" and "Rambling Man," Billy "Crash" Craddock had a number one with his rockabilly "Rub It In," Billy Swan's "I Can Help," a throwback rockabilly song reached number one, and John Denver, considered an interloper by many long-time fans, had a number one country hit with "Back Home Again." All of those guys let their hair grow long, although it wasn't down to their shoulders.

In 1975 Linda Ronstadt had a number one country hit with "When Will I Be Loved." Willie Nelson—who let his hair grow to his shoulders as he pushed the boundaries of country music— had his first number one hit with "Blue Eyes Crying in the Rain."

Waylon summed up the new beat and message of country music with his number one hit, "Are You Sure Hank Done It This Way." That year John Denver won the CMA's "Entertainer of the Year" award while Waylon Jennings was voted "Best Male Artist." By 1976, the "Outlaw movement" was in full swing as country artists put a heavy beat in their songs and let their hair grow long. The album *The Outlaws*, featuring Waylon, Willie Nelson, Jessi Colter and Tompall Glaser won the CMA's "Album of the Year" honors. The rednecks and the hippies finally found common ground in country music with long hair, marijuana and beer as they sang honky tonk songs.

Former pop artist Kenny Rogers' song, "Lucille" was voted CMA's "Song of the Year" in 1977. In 1979 Willie Nelson was voted CMA's "Entertainer of the Year" while "Devil Went Down to Georgia" by southern rockers The Charlie Daniels Band won "Single of the Year." George Jones became cool with young audiences with his soulful country singing and Loretta Lynn opened eyes and ears with her song "The Pill" about birth control. By the end of the 1970s, it wasn't your Grandpa's country music any more. In 1980 the film *Urban Cowboy*, starring John Travolta, took the cowboy off the horse and away from the ranch and put him in a pick-up truck and had him working in an oil refinery in Houston. Those cowboys didn't ride a real bull — it was mechanical — and the film launched a cowboy craze all across America. Even Motown's Smokey Robinson was spotted wearing cowboy boots.

Paul McCartney in Nashville

On Thursday, June 6, 1974, Paul McCartney and his family flew from Los Angeles to Nashville for a six week stay. His band, Wings, was scheduled to arrive the next day and McCartney stated, "We have a new drummer, Geoffrey Britton. He's a karate expert—has a black belt. I figure with those credentials he'll be able to whip the band in shape" and laughed at his comment.

McCartney said the reason he chose Nashville was because "I rather fancy the place. It's a musical center. I've just heard so much about it that I wanted to see for myself," adding that "We didn't come here to hide out" and plans to be available to the press for interviews, adding, with a smile, "Maybe we'll have you reporters out some evening for a party." [1]

McCartney stated he came to Nashville "to rehearse, relax and ride" and use it as a rehearsal base for his upcoming tour. McCartney stated he loved country music, "I was raised on it!" and "may record here. I don't know, it depends on how things go." [2]

McCartney, his wife Linda and daughters Heather (11), Mary [5] and Stella [3], landed at 8:30 in the evening and were met by TV crews and reporters in addition to about 50 fans. The McCartney group stayed on a farm, rented for $2,000 a week, owned by Tree songwriter and executive Curly Putnam (he had written "Green, Green Grass of Home" and "My Elusive Dreams"). Tree publishing executives Buddy Killen and Donna Hilley were at the airport, along with public relations executive Bill Hudson and McCartney Production executives to pick them up.

During 1969, when the other Beatles chose Allen Klein to manage them, McCartney insisted on being managed by his father-in-law, noted New York music attorney Lee Eastman. Eastman was also the attorney for Tree International and contacted Killen seven weeks before their arrival to arrange the visit. Eastman wanted the McCartneys to stay on a farm where they would not be hassled by fans and where his new group, Wings, could rehearse.

Curly and Bernice Putman owned a 133-acre farm in Lebanon, thirty miles east of Nashville, and Killen asked Putman if he would rent the farm for an amount that would allow them a vacation; Putman agreed and he and his wife went to Hawaii during the time the McCartneys stayed in his home.

The Tennessean reported McCartney stating they were there for "rehearsing, relating and riding"—which mean rehearsing the newly formed Wings band, mixing with the musical community and horseback riding, which they both enjoyed.

The McCartneys were the last to deplane, with the entourage headed by manager Brian Brooly, who carried daughter Mary when he got off the plane. Brooly was followed by Paul (in a jade green battle jacket and bright picture shirt" who emerged "smiling with his hand extended in a familiar two-finger salute." At the bottom of the flight stairs, McCartney paused and answered questions and posed for photographs before making his way through the terminal to a waiting limousine.

The article noted that Linda McCartney's first public role with McCartney was singing harmony on "Let It Be" and that she was an active photographer whose pictures were often used with McCartney interviews and albums and "will someday have a photography book out." The article also noted that she planned to one day release a single under the name "Suzy and the Red Stripes" "just for fun." [3]

Red O'Donnell in *The Banner* reported that on Wednesday, the day before the McCartneys arrived in Nashville, Ringo Starr told reporters in London "I'll bet anyone a thousand pounds ($2,400) that the Beatles will never play together again. Not this year, or for that matter, ever. We are all doing our own thing apart from everyone else. We are too busy to get together again."

According to O'Donnell, McCartney, when asked about the quote, agreed, stating "I'd bet as much, but I wouldn't raise his ante." [4]

Killen's group took them to Putman's farm, which was stocked with food and supplies requested by the McCartneys. Donna Hilley had received a list of foods and supplies to purchase — complete with brand names — and spent hours purchasing from the list. Among the things the McCartneys requested were "an orange squeezer-juicer because the family likes fresh orange juice each morning" as well as "31 flavors of ice cream, Dannon blueberry yogurt, raw sugar, smoked bacon, fresh blueberries, ripe watermelons, various cheeses, 100% maple syrup, and Pears soap," which Hilley could not find so Amino Pon soap was substituted. [5] (Pears soap is a translucent soap manufactured in England.)

Paul McCartney and Wings

After the Beatles officially broke up in 1970, McCartney released a solo album, *McCartney*. Much of the album was recorded alone in McCartney's home in St. John's Wood, London, although

"Maybe I'm Amazed," which became the most popular track on that album, was recorded at the Abbey Road studio. Another track, the beautiful "Junk," had been written when McCartney was in India with the Beatles but was never on a Beatles album.

The breakup of the Beatles caused Paul to retreat to his farm in Scotland, where he suffered a deep depression. During the time he was out of the limelight is when rumors ran rampant that he was dead.

McCartney's second album, *Ram*, credited to Paul and Linda McCartney, included guitarists David Spinozza and Hugh McCracken and drummer Dennis Seiwell. That album, released on May 17, 1971, included the hit singles "Uncle Albert/Admiral Halsey" and "Another Day." The album was recorded in New York during October and November, 1970, and finished in February the following year.

In 1971, McCartney decided to form a band and reportedly came up with the name "Wings" after praying for Linda, who was going through a difficult, life-threatening birth with their daughter, Stella. Drummer Denny Seiwell, who played on *Ram* joined and so did Denny Laine, a musician McCartney had known since the 1960s when Laine was with the Moody Blues and sang their hit "Go Now." (The Moody Blues were managed by Brian Epstein.) Their first album as Wings was *Wild Life*, released in December, 1971. In 1972 guitarist Henry McCullough joined the group, which released the singles "Give Ireland Back to the Irish" (banned by the BBC) and "Hi, Hi, Hi." The 1973 album *Red Rose Speedway* was released as Paul McCartney and Wings and had the hit single, "My Love."

In October, 1972 Wings recorded "Live and Let Die," the theme song for the James Bond film of the same name; the single was produced by former Beatles producer George Martin. In August, 1973, Seiwell and McCullough left Wings, so the group became, Paul, Linda and Denny Laine, who recorded *Band on the Run,* which had three hit singles, the album's title cut, "Jet" and "Helen Wheels."

In 1974, guitarist Jimmy McCulloch joined the band; he was formerly with the groups Thunderclap Newman and Stone the Crows. Drummer Geoff Britton also joined Wings and this was the group—Paul, Linda, Laine, McCulloch and Britton—who came to Nashville for rehearsals in June 1974. McCartney brought the group to Nashville to rehearse and bond for an upcoming tour.

The McCartneys at Opryland

On Sunday, June 16, a week after their arrival, the McCartney's visited Opryland Theme Park. At Opryland, Buddy Killen walked up to the admission booth, bought tickets and took the McCartney family inside, without notifying security and soon they attracted a large crowd who followed and wanted autographs. Paul was gracious and accommodating until the Opryland security force arrived to help.

The third annual "Grand Masters Fiddling Contest" was held that day and the McCartneys listened to the fiddlers. During intermission at the contest, Porter Wagoner and Dolly Parton performed. The paper noted that Killen, Irving Waugh, president of WSM, which owned the Grand Ole Opry and Opryland, and Opryland security cordoned off the McCartneys to give them protection from the fans. The McCartneys sat ten rows back from the left hand side of the stage. The paper stated that "the country music stars were the main attraction" and, when asked if the performers knew the McCartneys were in attendance, Waugh replied that he doubted that Grant Turner, WSM and Grand Ole Opry broadcaster who emceed the Fiddling Contest, knew who McCartney was.

Irving Waugh, who escorted the McCartneys through the park, noted that Paul "is a very gracious person. He is very cordial to the fans, always stopping for autographs and pictures with the girls and babies." A reporter noted that most of the audience did not recognize McCartney the first 45 minutes they were seated watching the fiddlers fiddle, but then a young man shouted, "Hey, Mr. McCartney" so he could take a picture. That let out the Big Secret.

Waugh also commented that many autograph seekers who requested McCartney's signature "didn't know who he was. They just knew he was a Beatle." The reporter stated that Linda McCartney had her camera and on several occasions left her seat to photograph the entertainers on stage. [1]

Nashville Banner reporter Bill Hance reported that "For a few fleeting seconds, the black-haired fair complected guy and his wife and three daughters looked like ordinary Johnny and June Citizen and family," adding "but it didn't take long for a couple of young, stray girls to recognize him, let out a squeal and cause word to travel faster than a brush fire."

During the show, which was Porter and Dolly's last show together, Dolly dedicated a song to Porter she had just written for him, "I Will Always Love You." Dolly left the Porter Wagoner Show after this concert and embarked on a solo career. After their performance, the McCartneys visited backstage, then visited the park before WSM President Irving Waugh came with his station wagon to take them out of Opryland at 4:15 p.m. [2]

After leaving the park, Killen offered to take the group to his home in nearby Donelson where they could relax by the pool. They readily agreed and Killen bought buckets of fried chicken on the way. After eating the chicken at the house, and before they had washed the gravy and grease from their hands, the children "began to jump up and down on the white crushed-velvet couches as if they were trampolines, stomping mashed potatoes into the fabric," stated Killen. "Each time one of them would touch the newly painted walls, a child-size oily handprint remained," adding "Paul and Linda were very lenient parents and didn't seem to notice the children's antics." [3]

Killen had recently decorated his home and "felt a little protective of the place" but did not discipline the children. He decided to take them for a ride to get them out of the house. The McCartneys waited outside while Killen activated the burglar alarm when he "heard the sound of breaking glass, immediately followed by a child hysterically screaming." Linda rushed back into the house and grabbed some towels. Four-year old Stella lay on the sidewalk, bloody from running through a glass door. Stella had forgotten her shoes and was running back into the house when she ran through the plate glass; she broke through the bottom, then the top half of the glass door fell down on her, cutting her arms and both legs. Meanwhile, the burglar alarm was blaring.

Killen got the group into his Cadillac and drove to a emergency treatment center. Inside the car was chaos; a young child crying with her parents trying to console her. [4]

An emergency room doctor took care of young Stella, stitching up her cuts. Nurses and doctors, alerted that Paul McCartney was there, came by, sneaking peeks.

The Sound Shop

Buddy Killen told Paul McCartney about his studio, Sound Shop, which was owned by Killen with Bob Montgomery, Bobby Goldsboro and Kelso Herston and located at 1307 Division Street, just off Music Row. The group purchased the studio from Danny Davis, who worked in A&R at RCA before he became a recording artist (Danny Davis and the Nashville Brass). "It was an old guitar factory," said engineer Ernie Winfrey. "It had pecky cypress walls, which come from cypress trees that had been under water so they had a lot of holes in them which were supposed to be good for sound absorption."

During his time in Nashville McCartney recorded six songs: "Hey Diddle," "Bridge on The River Suite," "Wide Prairie," "Walking in the Park With Eloise," "Send Me The Heart," "Sally G." and "Junior's Farm."

The McCartney Sessions

One evening, Paul and Linda McCartney with their road manager, Alan Crowder, dropped by the Sound Shop unannounced.

"When the McCartneys walked into the studio I wasn't expecting them," said Ernie Winfrey, an engineer at Sound Shop.

"They just walked in — they'd been in town just riding around. I was working with Buddy on a Paul Kelly album and Buddy introduced us and when he said 'Ernie Winfrey' they said 'Oh, Ernie the fastest milk man in the West!' I didn't know what they were talking about. It turned out that Benny Hill, a British comedian, had a record out called 'Ernie, The Fastest Milk Man in the West' about a milk man who has affairs with his female customers and he has to be pretty fast to get away. So they called me 'Ernie the fastest milk man in the West' the whole time they were here."

"In the entrance area of the studio was a frame that you could slide a poster board in and Buddy Killen always put up a poster board in that frame when anyone well known came into the studio," said Winfrey. "The idea was that the person would sign it. Paul and Linda filled the entire board. They drew caricatures of themselves and wrote little witticisms around it. They drew a picture of me with a little leather cap on that I had just gotten at the flea market. Beside my name they wrote 'the fastest milk man in the West.'"

Paul drew himself as an Ogre and wrote "Howdy, ya'll. My name is Paul McCartney. Ain't I handsome" and signed his name. Linda wrote under that "and some." Then she drew a picture of herself and wrote "Tougher than a ten cent steak." That was a phrase she had probably heard in Nashville. Linda also signed her name. This poster is currently at the Musicians Hall of Fame in Nashville.

The group came into the studio "almost every night during a two week period to record," according to Winfrey. They had no roadies — Paul carried his Rickenbacker bass into the studio while the others carried their own guitars. The drummer brought his drums but the rest of the band used the studio's amplifiers, although McCartney plugged his bass directly in to the board.

"The sound of Paul's bass was so tight from note to note, top to bottom," remembered Winfrey. "Everything was in a dynamic range like that. He was very easy to record. We recorded on an MCI board and for the drummer, who was in a booth, I put mics on the toms, the kick drum and the top and bottom of the snare, although I had to be careful of phasing when I did that. Generally I had two overheads on the drums—six mics in total. The rest of the guys were in the room facing each other. Paul always stood up in front of the piano and sang live into the mic as he played."

"It was obvious they were well rehearsed when they came in," said Winfrey. "It didn't take them long to record once they got into the studio, although it took them longer than Nashville studio players who usually record three or four songs in a three hour session."

"McCartney directed them when they ran down a song," said Winfrey. "He always knew what he wanted and gave instructions about certain licks and things he wanted on the songs. He even played the drums to show the drummer what he wanted. They seemed to know what they were supposed to play by the time they got into the studio but Paul would go around and tweak, sit down on the drums, maybe play a certain riff or fill he was looking for."

"Once, while they were recording, he went back to the old pump organ we had in the studio," said Winfrey. "He liked to experiment with sounds. He's very creative."

"Something that will always stay with me is the memory of him during the sessions playing bass and singing as we cut the tracks. Watching him standing and leaning into that mike reminded me of the 'Ed Sullivan Show' when he leaned into that mic, singing and playing at the same time. For the most part his scratch vocal is what you hear on the records. On 'Junior's Farm' and possibly 'Sally G.' I tried to do a side by side comparison with the record and I couldn't tell. If he did another vocal, it was so close to the original that I couldn't tell."

Winfrey did not keep the tape running during the session. When it was time to record a song, they recorded it so there isn't much studio chatter on those tapes. "There wasn't a lot of fixing or overdubbing, although there was more overdubbing and adding things," said Winfrey.

The sessions generally started at six or seven in the evening and went to ten or eleven—maybe a bit later—until they were done. "Buddy tried to keep everything undercover; he didn't publicize their being in town or when they would record but there was always a big crowd around the studio," said Winfrey. "Back then there was a chain link fence between our studio and the Hall of Fame Motor Inn and from front to back a crowd was there. We had Paul bring the limo—he always came and left in a limo but the band members rented cars and I think they drove them to the studio-- but he brought the limo around to the back entrance of the studio and he would get out and sign autographs as he moved through the crowd. But he kept moving so that kinda kept the crowd quiet and subdued because they were over-energized because it was him. After the session, there would still be a crowd out there." [1]

EINRE YERFNIW

There's a picture of Ernie with McCartney and the shirt Winfrey is wearing says EINRE YERFNIW—which is "Ernie Winfrey" spelled backwards.

"I had a crazy friend, Jeffrey Comanor that I had just done a session with. We had a few wild nights together out on the town and he had that shirt printed and when he gave it to me he said, 'Ernie, wear this to bed at night so when you get up in the morning and look in the mirror you'll know who you are.'"

Bridge on a River Suite

"Bridge on a River Suite" is "a strange little song," said Winfrey. They cut the original tracks in Paris and added horns in Nashville along with some other overdubs. The song is an instrumental.

Wide Prairie

The original tracks for "Wide Prairie" were recorded in Paris in November, 1973; the tracks were sent to Nashville where a horn section and fiddles by the Cates Sisters were overdubbed.

"On 'Wide Prairie' we slowed the track down and McCartney recorded the solo with his bass and when the track was sped up it sounded like a Duane Eddy guitar part," said Winfrey. "He played his bass in a higher register through a guitar amp with a tremolo," then added, "even though some of the songs may not be that great, there's always little bits and pieces that make them neat to listen to."

Paul sang lead on the first verse of "Wide Prairie" in a mock over the top southern country vocal, followed by a lead vocal by Linda after shifting tempo. It was released on an album titled *Wide Prairie* by Linda McCartney after her death in 1998.

Send Me The Heart

Paul McCartney threw down a challenge to Denny Laine of "who can write the best country song." McCartney wrote "Sally G." and Laine wrote "Send Me The Heart." That song probably should have won—but "Sally G." was the single. Denny Laine sang it while McCartney sang harmony.

"It's just a tear jerker country song," said Winfrey. "Lloyd Green played steel guitar and McCartney sang a high tenor harmony. His tenor was so pure, there was no effort at all involved in it. He just stood there and sang a perfect harmony; it was beautiful. He is a natural harmony singer. I thought his harmony singing was the best part of that song."

Sally G.

Buddy Killen took the McCartneys to dinner at the Captain's Table in Printer's Alley, a local hot spot with restaurants and clubs in an alley between Third and Fourth Avenues North. After dinner, they went to a club, The Western Room, where McCartney reportedly got the idea for a song, "Diane," named for local country local singer Diane Gaffney. McCartney decided to change the title to "Sally G."

On the way back to the farm, according to Killen, Paul and Linda began sketching out ideas for the song, "Sally G." In the song it mentions Printer's Alley. "We cut 'Sally G.' about mid-way through the session," remembered Winfrey. "It was obviously a song he wrote while he was in Nashville, inspired by a trip to Printer's Alley."

Lloyd Green played steel guitar and the Cates Sisters played fiddles on the song, an obvious attempt by McCartney to write a full blown country song.

Buddy Killen called Lloyd Green to play on the session "but Paul had asked for me," remembered Green. "I wasn't a Beatles fan, hadn't really listened to them, and I'd worked with the biggest of the big country acts but the Beatles were bigger than God. I just said, 'Sure I can do it, Buddy.'"

On July 10, 1974, Green was booked for sessions at 6 and 10 p.m. Earlier that day, McCartney had recorded "Eloise."

"I figured there'd be security and there'd be people there but there were huge crowds," said Green. "I drove down the side street to Sound Shop and as I tried to get in I found I couldn't. A cop came up to my car and he said, 'Who are you and what do you want? I can't let you in here.' I said, 'Well, I'm recording' and he said 'What's your name?' He had a pass list and my name was on the list. So he said 'O.K.' They had to clear people out of the driveway—there were several hundred people there. And there were more later; after the session they surrounded the place. I was finally able to park.

"I got my steel and amp out of the car and there were two cops at the first door to the studio. They asked 'Who are you' and I had to show them my I.D. There was another check list. Then I get to the final door into the studio and there's guys in suits, private security. There were two guys close to the door and I had to show my I.D. again and once I got past that into the studio it was real quiet, like a cocoon. It was wonderful after I had gone through three security checks."

Green first met Alan Crowder because "Paul didn't come out for a few minutes." Green chatted with Crowder and Buddy Killen "and a few minutes later Paul and Linda came out and he ran over and hugged my neck, said 'Man, I'm so glad you can do this with me. I love your playing. I've been listening to your instrumentals" and he named two or three he'd heard on the BBC. I said, 'Wow, that's impressive.'"

"I soon realized that he and Linda tried to live a normal life, in a vacuum really," said Green. "The Beatles were still God-like and Paul was the guy out there doing this stuff. John had become reclusive by 1974 and George was isolated in his mansion in England and into whatever religion he was into. Paul was a normal guy—and still is. Paul told me, 'Linda and I can walk down the street in London and not get hassled because we'll walk down the street like normal people. I'll have the baby in my arms. People might say 'hello' but they don't hassle us.' I didn't challenge him on that but I wondered if he had security with him. He claimed they were perfectly normal people and I had the feeling that's what they tried to do in this little cocoon with security around them. He wasn't pretentious; he was just a nice guy and an enormously talented man."

"We cut 'Sally G.' the first thing," remembered Green. "We had Johnny Gimble on fiddle on it, too. He was still excited about Chet Atkins and Floyd Cramer, especially Chet. He was like a fan.

That kinda startled me; the Beatles were the biggest thing on the planet and he's amazed by Chet, who didn't do sessions any more for other artists, just cut his own records.

McCartney played "Sally G." on the guitar while the musicians listened. "He's like a little kid in a lot of ways," said Green. "He signed everything and put a smiley face under it, like a child-like caricature. That was just supposed to be a little double entendre song, I suppose. We didn't spend much time recording it but we spent a lot of time talking and kinda absorbing the song and then he said 'Let's do it' and suddenly everybody's ready to cut. It wasn't a structured environment like a regular Nashville session. We only did the one song each session."

As they practiced "Sally G." McCartney "really liked what I was doing and gave me a lot of latitude on the song. He was excited—he'd never cut with a steel guitar before. We cut that song after we'd spent two or three hours on it and then took a break at nine o'clock. They had food catered in and we ate.

"Paul said, 'I want to talk to you' and we went over to a corner and he said, 'I've got this tour coming up. It's going to be two months. I want you to do the tour with me. We'll do 15 minutes, a country segment, with me playing bass, Denny Laine on guitar and Geoff Britton on drums. We'll do strictly country and there'll be a spotlight on you and the steel guitar and country music.'"

"People were always asking me about going on the road after I'd cut with them and some of them would get mad because I wouldn't go on the road with them. Don Williams quit using me on sessions because I wouldn't take the road job with him. So I didn't even think, I just reacted instinctively, I said, 'Paul, I can't do it—I'm too busy. I've got too many commitments. I know it would be fun but I can't do it. I appreciate the offer.' He didn't act offended, he just said, 'Oh, O.K., I understand.' Buddy Killen overheard us and he told me later, 'That's the biggest mistake you've ever made. Money is no object and this will help your career.' But I had a career doing sessions. It's only been in recent years have I've been thinking and regretting that a bit. I wouldn't want to have anything change in my life but I'd like to have done that two month tour." [1]

A year after the session, Green said in an interview that "the lyrics [to "Sally G."] were pretty basic, academic, and nonsensical, but the melody [gives] a totally different perspective of music, because here's a rock-oriented artist who's kind of flirted with country music." Green noted that McCartney "told me he'd always liked country music [but] it was the kind of thing you just didn't talk about when the Beatles were [at] the epitome of their fame."

Green stated that McCartney was "a very bright man, a very musically talented man" who wrote a melody "and it's got all these infusions of rock, folk, and country that's blended…He's got chords that a traditional country writer wouldn't put in, and he sequences the chords in places that they change. The chord structure changes at places where a traditional melody wouldn't be thought to change because of a different train of thought." Green added, "That's real good, because we get a different idea of how to construct melodies from somebody like that because here he was trying to write a country song, but he couldn't possibly write it with the same factors in mind that a regular country writer would because he doesn't have the same makeup or knowledge musically. He's approaching it from a totally different culture and angle and everything. It comes out sounding like a totally different thing—a new form of music." [2]

Hey Diddle

The tracks for "Hey Diddle" were recorded in England with McCartney playing all the guitar parts. The tape was shipped to Nashville. "It sounded like they mic'd Paul's foot—there wasn't a drum on the track," said Winfrey.

In Nashville, the group overdubbed vocals with Paul, Linda and Denny singing harmony. Through the years a number of rock critics have criticized Linda's singing but Winfrey said, "The harmonies she did on those songs sounded pretty darn good when her harmonies were blended in."

During that song, Paul played the ocarina, a woodwind instrument that looks something like a potato with a mouthpiece on the side and holes in the body. "It's notoriously out of tune," said Winfrey, "it's even out of tune with itself. But Paul played a melody on that thing and asked Lloyd Green to play a harmony part behind it on the steel guitar. It was so funny watching Lloyd bending those strings trying to stay in tune with an out of tune instrument." [1]

The fiddles on "Hey Diddle" were played by The Cates Sisters, Marcy and Margie, who had studied classical music at the University of Missouri and the Kansas City Conservatory of Music; they each received a Masters degree in Music in 1971. After graduation they moved to Nashville where they worked as studio singers and fiddle players. In 1972 they joined "The Jim Ed Brown Show" where they sang with Jim Ed as a threesome, recreating the Browns sound with tight harmonies as well as performing as a duo. At the Wembley Festival in London in 1973 they did a twin-fiddle version of "Orange Blossom Special," which brought down the house. During the time they recorded with McCartney, they recorded singles for MCA Records and had several songs on the country charts in the mid-and-late 1970s.

Lloyd Green on "Hey Diddle"

On the ten o'clock session, when they did "Hey Diddle," Paul pulled out "a strange looking instrument" and Green asked, "What is that?" "It's an ocarina," McCartney replied. "It's potato shaped. It's an old instrument." Green had never seen one.

"I'm not sure how it came up that he asked me to play harmony," said Green. "He's a smart guy. I don't remember if it was his idea or mine. I said 'We don't want it to sound too much like a steel guitar.' I needed to get in the same pitch level with the ocarina so I said, 'Just play it for a little while.' He played it for me and I kept processing it in my brain and re-setting my amp to try to get it into the range and tonal quality and we got pretty darn close. The difference was the pedal movement. He liked that idea and I thought it came off really cool."

Green observed that the Beatles were all good musicians but "Paul was by far the better musician. The bass he played on 'Hey, Diddle' is brilliant. He's not like any bass player I ever worked with. The way he phrased, the syntax, the phrasing, the notes, the timing—everything was different from a typical bass player in Nashville. On 'Sally G' he played much hipper than a Nashville bass player. You can hear the hipness." [1]

Chet Atkins and Paul

Paul McCartney and his family visited Chet Atkins at the guitarist's home in Nashville. According to Chet, "Paul called me and he and Linda came out to the house. He wanted to meet Jerry Reed and I had Jerry here too. We all visited, and talked about people I recorded and had hits with, like Elvis and Waylon Jennings, The Browns and Don Gibson and Paul knew all that stuff."

Chet and his wife, Leona, took the McCartney's out to dinner at a famous tourist court motel restaurant, The Loveless Café, that specialized in "meat and three" meals. (For the non-country readers, this term applies to restaurants that serve home cooked meals consisting of a meat and three vegetables.) Atkins bought McCartney a souvenir T-shirt! "I thought he might write a song about the place," said Atkins.

Back at Chet's home they "visited some more. He sang a new song he had written and I said, 'Do you mind if I record that and play it for my daughter?' and he said 'O.K.' I had a piano in the living room at that time, so I recorded it for her." Atkins said that McCartney "was telling about how he first started writing songs, and he said his Daddy (James) had a song called 'Walking in the Park with Eloise' and it was kind of a 'Darktown Strutter's Ball' type of song with a similar structure, and so I told him the best gift you could ever give your father would be to record that."

Atkins told McCartney that he "had recorded a tune my Dad wrote called 'Prancin' Filly' and my Dad made two or three hundred dollars off of publishing. He loved it! He had never had a song recorded before." Paul loved that story.

Chet Atkins was an avid reader and McCartney saw a book on his bookshelf, *Secrets of the Pyramids* and asked if he could borrow it. Before he left Nashville, McCartney brought the book back "and he scribbled in it and wrote me a note, and thanked me and later on he wrote a tune about the book and put it in a later album," said Chet. "*Rolling Stone* magazine later asked him where he got the idea, and he told them I loaned him the book." (The song was "Spirits of Ancient Egypt" on the *Venus and Mars* album.)

"He's always been nice to me," remembered Chet before his death. "Not long ago he had a video out on 'Michelle,' and at the beginning he told me that he wrote that song trying to make music like I make, which was probably a fib, but it was a good plug for me and I'm sure that's the way he meant it." [1]

Walking in the Park with Eloise

After visiting Chet Atkins at home, Paul called and asked him to set up a session to record "Walking in the Park with Eloise." Chet contacted pianist Floyd Cramer, guitarist and banjo player Bobby Thompson, fiddlers Vassar Clements and Johnny Gimble, and a horn section: George Tidwell on trumpet, Dennis Goode on trombone, Norm Ray on baritone saxophone and Billy Pruett on clarinet. On July 10, 1974, the group went into the studio, rehearsed the song a couple of times, then recorded it. The horns played their parts, then overdubbed, doubling the horn section. The arrangements were by Tony Dorsey, who had worked on the Paul Kelly sessions. McCartney was impressed enough to hire Dorsey as his music director for the Wings tour.

Wings drummer Geoff Britton played drums on that session while McCartney played bass, then overdubbed a washboard he played with thimbles. McCartney had found the washboard in a local antique shop. The song was recorded straight through although Chet Atkins, a perfectionist, wanted to do his part again before he was satisfied.

The song has a Dixieland Jazz feel about it. The recording was released under the name "The Country Hams." McCartney arranged to have the song played on the BBC on his father's birthday and called to tell him "Be sure to listen to the BBC today. You might be surprised at what you hear."

Paul & Chet & The Country Hams

"When I was growing up I'd always heard this little song when my Dad played 'Chicago' and all the other tunes he played," remembered Paul McCartney. "There was always this other little one that I thought was a 'Chicago.' I never knew anything about it. But then his friends would come over and I think I'd heard him once or twice saying, 'You know, this is one I made up,' and he'd play it to them, so I knew he'd done this, and I suppose it must have given me a little bit of confidence to try in writing my own stuff. 'Well, me Dad did one, maybe I could do it.'

"So years, years, years later, when I was in Nashville, I mentioned it to Chet Atkins, who I'd met out there and I'm a big fan of, and he said, 'Why Paul, that's real interesting' and he's such a ..he is the country gentleman, Chet, just such a lovely man, so unassuming and a real great fella. I mean, just quickly I'll tell you while we were there we went to dinner with him, and this little kid came round. It was at a place called The Loveless Motel, and he'd take us for all the peach preserve and all that—'Get that down your neck, Paul, that's home cooking!' They were doing that with us. And the little kid came up, and he got my autograph, and he got Linda's and he went round to get Chet's, but he kind of looked like he wasn't quite sure whether Chet was a celebrity or not, and he said, 'Can I have yours too?' and Chet said 'Oh no, you don't want mine. I'm just old folk!' And that's how he is. He really plays it down so much."

"Anyway, I was talking to him just casually about my Dad having written this song, and somehow we cooked up the idea. We said, 'Wouldn't it be great just to record it, and we'll play it to my Dad and I'll say, 'Hey Dad, this is Chet Atkins playing on your record.' And he said, 'I'll tell you what, I'll get Floyd along, Floyd Cramer, so it was incredible—great, yeah! We had Geoff Britton, the drummer out of the group at the time, and me on bass, Chet on guitar and Floyd on piano. And we did this little instrumental and we called ourselves The Country Hams, and I was telling my Dad about it. I said 'We're going to do it and you know that song you wrote Dad?' He said 'No, son, I've never written a song.' I said, 'You did, you wrote—we called it 'Walking in the Park with Eloise.' He said, 'No son, I've never written one..I've made one up.'"

"You know, it was just that old-fashioned way of thinking about it. I said, 'We're calling that writing these days, Dad, you know, making up is the same thing.' Just because he couldn't physically write the notes down he didn't think he'd written it. So that was great, and we gave him..I sold him a copy of it!"[1]

Junior's Farm

"Junior's Farm' was one of the last songs the group recorded and the title came because Curly Putnam's nickname was "Junior." Before the session, Alan Crowder pulled Winfrey aside and asked him if he could cut rock'n'roll. Winfrey, whose musical roots were in Rhythm and Blues, said "I sure hope so."

"It was funny to me that he would inquire about that," said Winfrey. "It was like if anybody did country music they couldn't possibly do rhythm and blues or rock'n'roll. Buddy Killen and I had been working on Paul Kelly's album—it was R&B--and they'd heard some of the stuff we'd been doing. Of course, he might have just been messing with me."

On the Sound Shop tape you hear Paul say, "Are we ready? Ready Ernie? Let's cut it" then he counted off "one, two, three, four" and Jimmy McCulloch hit that opening riff, then Paul stepped to the microphone and sang the song straight through. At the end of the song, Paul is heard saying, "Sounded good to me, that one!"

"On 'Junior's Farm' we did maybe four or five takes," said Winfrey. "We never used more than a roll of tape on any given one- they were well rehearsed before they came in."

"Geoff Britton was a really good drummer, an excellent drummer," remembered Winfrey. "But I think he was too straight for them. He didn't smoke, didn't drink, didn't do anything except play drums. The next thing I knew they'd hired Joe English, which was a kinda funny thing with their names. From Britton to English. I guess they liked people with British names." [1]

Chet Atkins and Beatles Songs

Chet Atkins recorded sixteen Beatles songs. Since the Beatles albums released in the United States differed from those released in England, Chet heard the Beatles songs first from their American albums on Capitol. On his *Picks on the Beatles* album Atkins recorded instrumental versions of "I Feel Fine," "Yesterday," "If I Fell," "Can't Buy Me Love," "I'll Cry Instead," "Things We Said Today," "Hard Day's Night," "I'll Follow the Sun," "She's a Woman," "And I Love Her," "Michelle" and "She Loves You."

"She Loves You," was a single (#1 for two weeks) and on *The Beatles' Second Album*, on Capitol in the United States. "Can't Buy Me Love" (#1 for five weeks) and "Hard Day's Night" (#1 for two weeks) were both singles and were released on the *Hard Day's Night* album.

The *Hard Day's Night* album was released in the United States with eight Beatle songs from the film of that name with four orchestral arrangements of those songs. Their next American album on Capitol, *Something New*, contained five songs from the *Hard Day's Night* album and six additional songs so "If I Fell," "I'll Cry Instead" and "And I Love Her" were on the American *Hard Day's Night* as well as the *Something New* albums. "Things We Said Today" was on the *Something New* album, which was released in July, 1964. None of those songs were singles but they received enough airplay off the albums from disc jockeys that they made the Hot 100 chart ("If I Fell" #53; "And I Love Her" #12; and "I'll Cry Instead" #25).

From the album *Beatles '65*, released in December, 1964, Atkins recorded "I Feel Fine," "I'll Follow the Sun," and "She's a

Woman." "I Feel Fine" (#1 for three weeks on the *Billboard* chart) and "She's a Woman" (#4) were on a two sided single.

"Yesterday" was a single (#1 for four weeks in 1965) and was released on The Beatles *Yesterday and Today* album in June, 1966. "Michelle" was on the *Rubber Soul* album, released in December, 1965.

On Chet Atkins' album *It's a Guitar World*, released in 1967, he recorded the Beatles song, "For No One" which was released on their *Revolver* album in August 1966. On that album he also recorded "A Taste of Honey," which was included on the Beatles' Vee Jay album *Introducing the Beatles*. Atkins also recorded "What'd I Say" on that album, which was a popular song for the Beatles during their live performances in Germany and at the Cavern in Liverpool.

On his *Solid Gold '68* album, Chet recorded "Lady Madonna," a single that reached #4 on *Billboard's* Hot 100 chart in 1968; that song was also on the Beatles' *Hey Jude* album, released in February, 1970.

Chet Atkins' album *Lover's Guitar* contained "Those Were The Days," a single by Mary Hopkin in 1968 (#2) which was produced by McCartney for the Beatles' label, Apple. Atkins' *Solid Gold '69* album contained "Blackbird" from the Beatles *White Album*, released in November, 1968, and "Hey Jude," a number one single for nine weeks for the group in 1968-1969; this song later appeared on the *Hey Jude* album. The *Me and Jerry* album Atkins recorded with Jerry Reed contained the George Harrison song, "Something," a Beatles single in 1969 (#3 for two weeks) which was on their *Abbey Road* album.

The *Chet on the Road—Live* album in 1975 featured a Beatles medley of "Something" and "Lady Madonna." Chet Atkins' album, *And Then Came Chet*, released in 1979, contained a Beatles medley of "If I Fell," "For No One," "Something" and "Lady Madonna."

On the album *Country—After All These Years,* released in 1981, Chet Atkins recorded McCartney's song, "Let 'Em In," which was a single (#3 for four weeks) on the *Wings At the Speed of Sound* album. In his *Solid Gold Guitar* album, released in 1982, Atkins included four previously recorded Beatles songs, "Yesterday," "A Hard Day's Night," "And I Love Her" and "Things We Said Today." This was an album compiled by RCA after Atkins left that label and joined CBS. On his 1984 album *A Man and His Guitar*, Atkins recorded a Beatles medley of "If I Fell"/"For No One"/"Something"/"Lady Madonna." In the *Collector's Series* and *The Romantic Guitar*, both from RCA, "Yesterday" is included; that song and "Michelle" have been included on a number of Chet Atkins albums compiled by RCA after he left the label.

Chet Atkins began recording for Columbia in 1982 and on his 1988 album, *Chet Atkins, C.G.P. (Certified Guitar Player)* he recorded John Lennon's "Imagine," a single from Lennon (#3 for two weeks) in 1971.

On the import album, *Masters*, Atkins performed the Beatle's "I'll Follow the Sun," which came from the *Beatles '65* album, "Yesterday," "Michelle" and "Hey Jude." On the album *The RCA Years: 1947-1981*, Chet Atkins included "Junk," the Paul McCartney song on his first solo project, McCartney, released in 1970.

Atkins also accompanied Suzy Bogguss on "All My Lovin'" on the album *Come Together: America Salutes the Beatles*.

Chet Atkins was a Beatles fan, proven by the number of Beatle songs he recorded during his career. He was also a friend of Paul McCartney and when Atkins died, McCartney sent a huge floral wreath to his home.

Linda and Dixie

Buddy Killen and Donna Hilley felt that someone should be a "Girl Friday" for Paul and Linda during their time in Nashville and sent one of their Tree employees, Dixie Gamble, to the studio to meet them. When Dixie arrived at the studio she was met by Alan Crowder, who told her "Linda doesn't allow any women in the studio." "Why?" asked Dixie. "Because she's very jealous," replied Crowder.

"I was a single Mom with two kids making next to nothing at Tree," remembered Dixie, "and I was afraid of losing my job if I didn't do this. I asked Alan to tell Linda that and he said 'You might have better luck if you ask her to go shopping.'" Dixie agreed and Alan went back in, asked Linda if she'd like to go shopping and she agreed."

When Dixie arrived at the studio Linda was darning one of Paul's socks, with it stretched over a Coke bottle. "I thought surely they could afford a pair of socks," said Dixie. "I was shaking when I was there and in my catty Southern girl way I thought 'WOW! He's more beautiful than his pictures!' when I saw Paul."

Dixie led Linda out to her old yellow Toyota and they got in and headed to Pangaea, a shop in Hillsboro Village. "We just fell in with girl talk," remembered Dixie, "but at the same time I'm thinking I'VE GOT LINDA MCCARTNEY IN MY CAR!' But we talked about children and being a mom and breast feeding—how long to do it—and boyfriends and husbands and how do you know when you've found the right one. Just girl talk." At Pangaea, Linda "bought an enormous amount of stuff. I think shopping was her thing."

The children weren't with them at the studio. "They had one or two nannies so the kids stayed at the farm," said Dixie. "Linda would call sometimes and say she was looking for something and I'd tell her where to find it. Sometimes I picked her up but sometimes she drove. She and Paul both drove themselves around—Paul like to drive. They were not ostentatious."

Whenever they went into a store or out in public, Linda was always recognized "but there was that Nashville boundary with celebrities," said Dixie, "so she wasn't hounded." It was a different story when the McCartneys went to the Tree offices because "out in the parking lot it was full of people wanting an autograph," said Dixie. "There were guys wanting Paul to sign their guitars and just a huge crowd there."

Paul and Linda "were really loose hippies," said Dixie, "and I didn't know how to be a loose hippie. The children ran around naked and whenever they had to go to the bathroom, they just did it where the urge hit. They destroyed Curly Putnam's house—drew on the wall with crayons and just wrecked the place." [1]

Bobby Braddock

Bobby Braddock has been one of Tree Publishing's consistent hit songwriters. At the time Paul and Linda McCartney were in Nashville, Braddock was known for writing "D-I-V-O-R-C-E" which Tammy Wynette recorded; later he wrote "Golden Ring" for George Jones and Tammy Wynette, "Time Marches On" by Tracy Lawrence, "I Wanna Talk About Me" by Toby Keith, "People Are Crazy" by Billy Currington and the classic "He Stopped Loving Her Today" (written with Curly Putnam for George Jones.)

Braddock told Buddy Killen how much he loved the Beatles and would like to meet Paul and Killen replied that Paul and Linda were coming by Tree late the next afternoon to go to dinner at the Loveless Café with Buddy and Chet Atkins. Buddy told Braddock that he would ask the McCartneys to come by early so he could meet them.

"The McCartneys drove up in a rental car," remembered Braddock. "Paul was wearing a leisure suit and Linda was wearing a peasant dress. When Buddy introduced him as 'Paul,' I said, 'Oh, Paul Smith, the bluegrass guy, right?' just being silly. Paul thought that was very funny and playfully punched me on the arm, so we hit it off from the start. He asked me a lot of questions about Nashville and I asked him some Beatles questions, such as 'Did you really record Sgt. Peppers on four tracks?' his answer being 'Yes.'"

"He and Linda seemed pleasantly surprised to encounter someone in country music who knew all about their current Wings album, *Band On the Run*," continued Braddock. "After chatting for a few minutes, Buddy said they needed to go pick up Chet. "Paul asked me, 'BO-bee, you're going with us aren't you?' I could tell that Buddy was about to have a stroke. I don't think he wanted one of his writers to elbow in on his superstar elbow-rubbing, so I quickly said, 'Oh no, I'm a big fan and just wanted to meet you guys.' Linda, who struck me as a beautiful person inside and out, sweetly said, 'Well we will be seeing you again, won't we?' I told her 'I sure hope so.' That was the last time I saw them but I will never forget how nice they both were. Buddy pitched a couple of my songs to Paul, but why in the world would the greatest pop/ rock songwriter of all time record some hillbilly's song?" [1]

Dixie's Party

Dixie had to entertain the Wings band so she set up a party at her friend, Martha Sharp's house. Martha was a well-known songwriter who wrote "Single Girl" and "Born a Woman," both hits for Sandy Posey, and "Come Back When You Grow Up Girl," which was a hit for Bobby Vee.

"That band was hell on earth," said Dixie. "Their recklessness was frightening—they were so wild! At the party, Jimmy McCulloch was dancing on top of Martha's huge, vintage glass top coffee table. They were jumping into the pool—completely plowed. You didn't know if somebody had drowned or not. I had been around music business parties in Nashville but this was complete out of control chaos with cocaine and heroin and who knows what else." [1]

THE BEATLES AND COUNTRY MUSIC

Jimmy McCulloch

Guitarist Jimmy McCulloch "was a mess," remembered Ernie Winfrey. McCulloch was 21 at the time of the Nashville visit and had formerly been in the bands One in a Million, Thunderclap Newman and the Stone Crows.

"He was only about five feet tall and kinda cocky in his attitude," said Winfrey, "probably a result of being so short. So he overcompensated in every way possible. He came into the studio one night when Buddy and I were in there mixing. He sorta threw his hand up when he walked in and then sat down on the couch, which was below the level of the board so we couldn't see him. We were mixing and all of a sudden I saw a small glass Coke bottle arc up and go towards the window between the control room and studio. It hit the glass, which was at an angle, so it didn't break but fell off. Buddy jumped up, grabbed Jimmy by the arm and said, 'You need to leave' and led him out the front door. He was really snockered. He could barely stand and Buddy actually shouldn't have made him leave but he got in his car and the cops got him and took him down to Night Court. I believe he came before Judge Norman, who was a friend of Buddy's. They called Buddy in the middle of the night at his home and he got out of bed and went downtown. The Judge told Buddy what all they had found on him and it was everything you could think of--prescription drugs, marijuana, cocaine—everything. I heard that the Judge said 'I'm going to let him go, but if he ever comes back to Nashville I'll put him in jail.'"

There had been problems with McCulloch earlier during a recording session. "Buddy had ambitions, I think, to produce

McCartney," said Winfrey, "so Buddy was in the studio while they were running down the first song and it wasn't working out the way that Buddy thought it should so he hit the talk back button and said, 'Jimmy, why don't you sit this one out and then we can overdub your part.' When Buddy said that, McCulloch slammed his guitar down into his holder and walked out of that studio in a huff. I don't think he came back that day. He was hard to deal with."

"After that encounter with Jimmy on that first day, Paul apparently had a talk with Buddy," said Winfrey. "Then Paul came to me later and said 'This is how it's going to be. The only people I want in the studio are us and you.' Buddy never did show his face again during a session. Paul figured out what was going on and he was very polite when he told Buddy but I think he suggested he was a little disruptive with things."

McCulloch remained with Wings for several years and wrote the music to "Medicine Jar" on the *Venus and Mars* album and "Wino Junko" on the *Wings at the Speed of Sound* album. Colin Allen wrote the lyrics to those songs and McCulloch sang the lead vocal. McCulloch left Wings in 1977 to join Small Faces for a tour, then joined several other bands before he died in 1979, at the age of 26, from a heroin overdose in London.

Except for McColloch, "All the other guys seemed to be pretty together," remembered Winfrey. "I never saw Paul smoke or drink anything until after we got through recording. At the end of a session, he and Linda would pour a shot of Johnny Walker Red in a glass of Coke and occasionally they would light up a joint. But he never did anything while he was working. He was all business in the studio."

"Paul and Linda just seemed almost child-like in their attitude," remembered Winfrey. "They figured they could go anywhere and nobody would bother them. And they had all these kids with them." [1] (Their son, James, was not born until 1977).

Linda and Paul

Dixie was struck by the fact that when Paul addressed Linda he "called her Mummy! It was like he was one of her kids. Linda had these large, pendulous breasts with no bra, long skirt, her legs weren't shaved—long hair on them—and she was completely nurturing. He was totally devoted. The way he looked at her was worshipful, like 'you are my everything.' He had lost his mother when he was young and he transferred all of that to Linda and she accepted it."

"She was very jealous," said Dixie, "and she didn't want to let him out of her sight. That's why she traveled with Wings." At the studio during the recording of "Eloise," there was "a who's who of great Nashville musicians in the studio" and Linda and Dixie were in the control room, sitting on the couch in front of the window. Linda was darning when Paul said "'Mummy, time to do your part' and Linda got up and walked into the studio, totally unconcerned that these were great musicians. I've got to give her credit for courage. It didn't bother her in the least. She didn't care; she just put down her darning and went in."

That was the session where Chet Atkins played guitar. "Paul was really enamored of Chet," said Dixie. "He talked about him and had so much respect for him."

"She took a camera everywhere," remembered Dixie, "and she had a really good eye. At the end of 1976, Linda sent Dixie a Christmas card and a book of photos, *Linda's Pix for '76.*

"Linda was a real Earth Mother," said Dixie, "and she and Paul were really part of the '70s, just hippies who embraced all those hippie ideas. They were like little kids, just oblivious and there was an innocence. They were living in their own paradigm and when you have that much money and that much power, you can do that." Looking back at that time, Dixie stated, "They must have done something right because all those kids turned out fine. Stella is a major fashion designer." [1]

Danny Ealey: Super Fan

Before Paul McCartney arrived in Nashville there was a small article in the newspaper that stated there was a "rumor" that Paul McCartney would soon visit. "I was determined that if Paul McCartney was coming to Nashville, then I was going to find him," said Danny Ealey, who was a nineteen year old resident of Cookeville, Tennessee, about 90 miles east of Nashville, who worked at a gas station. A few days later he saw a picture in the newspaper of McCartney getting off the plane at the Nashville airport.

Ealey then plotted a scheme. He called Chris Charlesworth at the New York office of *Melody Maker* magazine (it was a cold call—Charlesworth had never heard of Ealey) and told him he was a reporter and would like to be a stringer to cover Paul McCartney's visit to Nashville. "I talked them into letting me do it," said Ealey. "I had absolutely no experience but they didn't know that. So they sent me a letter of authorization which gave me some credence."

Ealey heard that McCartney and his group were staying "in a doctor's house that looked like a mansion with a swimming pool on Franklin Road in Lebanon," about 30 miles east of Nashville. On a Sunday, Ealey was "driving up and down Franklin Road and I don't see anything but a long road. I don't see anything. I'm almost ready to give up but there's one guy walking on the road and he's a farmer with overalls on. I didn't want to stop and ask him anything because I thought this guy would know nothing but he was the only guy out there so I stopped. I said, 'Sir, I'm looking for a house on Franklin Road, a mansion that's a doctor's house that has a swimming pool.' He said, 'No, there's no house like that on Franklin Road.' I said, 'Well, is there a mansion-a big, big house. He said 'nothing with a swimming pool.' Then I said, 'one of the Beatles is supposed to be staying there.' I figured he didn't even know who the Beatles were. He said, 'You mean those fellers from England?' and I said, 'Yeah.' He said, 'They're up at Junior Putnam's place.' I said, 'Where's that?' He said, 'It's just up the road around the bend. But he don't have no swimming pool.'"

"I was so excited," continued Ealey. "You've got to understand, Paul McCartney is my hero. I've been watching him since 'The Ed Sullivan Show'! I look through books, find articles, it consumes my life! The next thing I'm pulling up in the driveway and Jimmy McCulloch and Denny Laine are sitting under a shade tree. There's no air conditioning in that house so they're sitting outside. Inside it's just mattresses on the floor. I get out and introduce myself and pull out the letter from *Melody Maker* so I could drop a name. I said, 'I've got a Les Paul in the car. Do you want to see it?' because a guitar will break the ice. So they said, 'Yeah, let's see it.' So I get this Les Paul out and Denny's playing it and I'm sitting there practically hyper ventilating and I said, 'Hey, Denny, could you show me the opening lick to 'Band on the Run?' Denny goes, 'Oh, man, I don't want to play no guitar today." Jimmy said, 'Hey man, I'll show you' so Denny hands him the guitar and he shows me the opening lick to 'Band on the Run.' So I became friends with them and was hanging out."

Every day, Denny worked at the gas station in Cookeville on Jefferson Street from 6 a.m. until 2 p.m. As soon as he finished "I got in my Ford Torino station wagon and I made it to Lebanon in about 20 minutes. I was in heaven every day with those guys. I took down magazines and albums for them and they could tell that I was a huge, huge fan."

"When I was first there, Paul's step daughter, Heather, who was 12, came down on a horse with Rusty, the German shepherd and tried to run me off," said Ealey. "I had Keith Bilbrey's tape recorder hung over my shoulder when I saw her coming and I sorta flipped it around behind me. It was running and you can hear the horse trotting and the German shepherd panting and she said, 'My mother sent me to find out what you're doing here and if you're not supposed to be here to get rid of you' and I said, 'I'm friends of Geoffrey, the drummer' and she said, 'Well, why don't you go over by that gate or go out to lunch or something.' She was really nasty. I said, 'Well, Paul McCartney is practicing and I want to hear him. I'm not bothering anyone' and she said, 'Yes, you are, actually. Isn't it good that they have something nice now and then?' I've got all that on tape."

One day, Ealey was sitting at the table in the guest house while they ate an afternoon breakfast. "I was still amazed that people would eat baked beans and ketchup for breakfast," said Ealey. "I said, 'Why did you guys shave your beards off that you had in Nigeria?' McCulloch looked at the other guys and said, 'He knows more about us than we do!' We just clicked; they liked me and I liked them—we had a rapport. I took gifts down every day for the kids—t-shirts and liquor for the band. I showed up one day with a duffle bag that this friend of mine gave me that had artillery simulators in it—he was in the National Guard. So I brought 'em down and showed 'em what they were and said, 'Here guys, maybe you can have some fun.' They were bored a lot of times during the day. A few days later I drove back up and it's very hot and Alan Crowder, Paul's right hand man, is out at the gate with his shirt off with a hammer and he's working at the gate. It's tremendously hot. I pulled up right beside him and asked, 'Alan, what are you doing?' He said, 'Paul is really pissed off!' I said 'Why?' He nodded his head towards the guest house and said, 'They blew up the mailbox.' I knew I was responsible for that but didn't want to talk about it so I rolled up the window and drove on up to the guest house."

On Monday, June 17, Ealey was visiting the band "and the guys told me that it was best if I didn't come the next day. They didn't tell me why but I said 'O.K.' and didn't go," remembered Ealey. On Tuesday it was Paul's birthday but an electric storm came up that day. "The next day I go back and I notice there's some activity that's not the norm. They're busy getting stuff out of the car and I saw a case of champagne. It was a birthday party for Paul but it was very low key for the stature of a Beatle. Probably any party I've been to in my life has been bigger than that. Very low key. They needed someone to work the gate and I was the only one there so they asked me to do it. They said, 'If you do it, then we'll take you down and you can hang out with Paul.' So I said, 'What do I do?' They said, 'Let the people in who are supposed to be here and don't let people in who aren't supposed to be here.' I said, 'Who's supposed to be here?' and they said, 'Chet Atkins, Jerry Reed and Roy Orbison.' Paul wanted those guys to watch the gate but they wanted to go to the party."

Chet Atkins came in a white Cadillac and Jerry Reed was with him. They came and soon left but Roy Orbison came and stayed.

"I'm up at the gate where they're having the little get-together and I can see them," said Ealey "and, as the sun starts to set, I figured Paul would send one of the band members up to get me but I look and Paul is walking through the field towards me. I had bought Paul a shirt—found it in a store in Cookeville—and it was a black shirt with a lot of embroidery in the front. And I'm sitting there watching him and he comes up wearing the shirt I gave him and he said, 'You're the one who left a bass guitar, right?' And I said, 'Yes, I am.' He said, 'You're not going to do something silly like try to give that to me, are you?' Those were his first words to me and I said 'No.' So we walked back together down to the party and he introduces me to Roy Orbison. Back before the Beatles hit here they were on a tour playing warm up for Roy Orbison, who was headlining. Hey, it don't get any better than that!"

"Paul would stop often at the gate; actually they didn't have a gate, it was an entrance. Linda would be with him in the car. One day I took Billy Dyer, one of my buddies with me. He was a gigantic Beatles fan and I'm going down there every day so shouldn't I, at some time, invite my best buddy to go? After I'd been there a number of times and had sorta accomplished what I wanted to do I said to Billy, "Hey, wanna go meet Paul?' He said, 'Yeah, let's go' so we get about half way to Lebanon in my old Torino station wagon and I have a flat tire on the Interstate. Just horridly hot. As I put the last lug nut on I looked up at Billy, who's about six foot four, and I'm sweating profusely and I said, 'Do you wanna go back?' Billy said, 'Ah, man, we might as well gone on.' So I threw the lug wrench in the car and we went down there."

"Now in 1974 cameras were either cheap, pieces of crap or they were pretty expensive. There wasn't a lot of in-between. I had this little 16 mm camera with me and you had to remember what frames you had on your film. So we get there and Billy's outside in the yard, I go in and talk to the band and Billy runs in and says, 'Paul is coming down the driveway.' You know how Barney Fife fumbles and gets all freaky with his bullet when he's trying to put it in his gun? Well, that's what I was doing with the camera because I couldn't remember if I had any more frames left. So I grabbed a new roll and snapped it in quick and I ran out in front of the car. The pictures show me right in front of Paul's car and there's the hood ornament right in front of me. Paul rolled down the window and said, 'How're you doing, Dan?' This is Billy's first encounter with him. I thought 'Wow, Paul McCartney knows my name!' I've always thought that if I ever write a book about all this then that'll be the title: 'Paul McCartney Knows

Your Name.' Billy poses with Paul, Linda's in the car, then I get up there and Billy takes a picture of me and Paul with Linda in the car. Later, Billy told me that I'd jumped right in front of the car. I didn't believe him but when I looked at those pictures there's the hood ornament right in the middle of the bottom of the picture."

Easley remembered that the band asked him if he knew a steel guitar player. Danny said, "Yeah, Pete Drake." The band members replied, "Paul doesn't want to use Pete because he played on George's stuff. I thought that was interesting. Just because he played with George, Paul didn't want to use him."

Danny Ealey received an additional thrill two years later, in 1976, when Paul McCartney wore the shirt he gave him during his "Wings Over America" tour.

Ealey never wrote any stories for *Melody Maker* because "the guys in the band came to me and said, 'Paul hates reporters and he will not be happy if he finds out you're a reporter.' I said 'I'm not a reporter and I don't care about writing anything. I just want to be here.' *Melody Maker* never pressed me to come up with an article. I contacted them just for my scheming so I could drop a name or a letterhead. I still have that letter; it's framed in my home." [1]

Conflicts

There were conflicts and problems with the group while on the farm. Danny Ealey remembers that he felt some tension in the group after he arrived one day. When Alan Crowder came to the guest house where the band was staying, Ealey asked him, "What's going on?" Crowder reportedly replied, "Paul McCartney is a superstar and he expects to be treated that way."

"I got the impression they had a problem with the guys living in the guest house on Curly's farm," said Ernie Winfrey. "I don't know what kind of trouble they got into but eventually they had to move them into the main house. I understood they let the girls run around naked and anytime they felt like going to the bathroom they just did it there. Maybe they were used to doing that in Scotland on their farm. From what I understand Curly had to do a lot of repair work on that house."

Buddy Killen also had to do repair work on his home after the McCartney's left. "Buddy had his living room done all in white — white carpet, white furniture, white walls, white everything," said Winfrey. "He was real particular about that place and the kids were jumping on the furniture in their bare feet. Then one of the girl's ran through a glass door and bled a lot. He told me about that when it happened."

The McCartney group did not have an extensive familiarity with country music or country artists but "They were somewhat familiar with the real big names in country music, like Chet Atkins, Johnny Cash and Buck Owens," said Winfrey. "They visited Chet and Johnny Cash but I don't remember them talking much about country music. And Paul never mentioned the Beatles. They were going through a tough time and that was a subject you just didn't bring up."

The McCartneys Visit Johnny Cash

During his time in Nashville, McCartney visited Johnny Cash at the singer's home in Hendersonville, where Cash asked if he would write some songs for him.

"I don't remember much about that visit because I was quite young," said John Carter Cash. "But I remember they sat up for a long time trading songs." [1]

In a press conference, McCartney acknowledged that "he had made several promises to write songs for several Nashville musicians although he had doubts about keeping them. 'The trouble is that since I've been here I promised a lot of people I would write songs for them,' said McCartney. 'It's amazing the people who want songs—like Johnny Cash and Charlie Rich. You'd think they'd have plenty of good material but they all tell us that they don't have enough good songs.'" [2]

Saying Good-bye to Nashville

Before they left Nashville, McCartney held a press conference at the Putnam farm. The McCartneys were relaxed, with Paul in bare feet wearing faded blue jeans and a loose fitting satin shirt while Linda wore a blue skirt and checkered shirt with home embroidery on the shoulders. Their children were asked to stay inside during the interview but, toward the end, came outside to play in the yard. Linda stated that the children are "always running around naked, streaking," but they had clothes on during the interview. Those who encountered the McCartneys noted their parenting was very "relaxed" and the kids were often barefooted; there did not seem to be a lot of parental discipline extended to the McCartney children.

"I've got a farm in Scotland," Paul stated. "You're not the only people who have farms, you know. Back in Scotland, we're country people in our own way." McCartney made it clear that "any recording was just incidental to the visit" because most of the time "was spent rehearsing with his group Wings, jamming with Nashville musicians and just enjoying the countryside." [1]

Leaving Nashville

Alan Crowder, Paul's personal assistant, had the burden of making sure everything ran without a hitch. Dixie and Alan talked and "one part of him hated that job but the other part was so devoted so he did it. Denny said that one time in the middle of a cold winter night in New York City Alan had to go out and find a watermelon."

"Alan was a nervous wreck when it came time to leave," remembered Dixie. "Paul wanted to buy a motorcycle and Alan went with him to buy it. It was a big Harley type thing and Paul wanted to drive it all the way back to New York. Alan had the responsibility of getting Paul and Linda back to New York safe and I thought Alan was going to have a complete nervous breakdown, muttering 'I have to talk him out of this.'" Dixie suggested that he let Paul ride the motorcycle for ten or fifteen miles on Interstate 40 and then he might want to put it away. That's what they did and that's what worked." [1]

Credits

On the official credits for the recordings made at the Sound Shop, Nashville was never mentioned because McCartney did not have a "Work Permit" to record in the United States. McCartney brought his group to Nashville to rehearse for a Wings tour and had not planned to do any actual recordings. However, it was never a secret that the songs were recorded in Nashville. After the group left, the Master tapes were shipped to London where Geoff Emerick mixed them. "Junior's Farm" and "Sally G." were issued back to back on a single.

Lloyd Green with Paul in France

Ringo's first two albums, released in 1970, were *Sentimental Journey* and *Beaucoups of Blues;* this was followed by his commercially most successful album, *Ringo*, which contained several hit singles, then *Goodnight Vienna*, after which he left Capitol/EMI and signed with Atlantic. In October, 1976, Ringo's *Rotogravure* album was released and the following year *Ringo The 4th* was released. Those albums were not commercially successful and Ringo was dropped by Atlantic. He signed with the Portrait label, a CBS Records affiliate for his album *Bad Boy*, which also did not sell well.

Ringo wanted to give up recording but McCartney visited him in Monte Carlo, where he was living and, with the further support of his future wife, Barbara Bach, encouraged him to do another album. Ringo reportedly told McCartney he needed a hit song and McCartney agreed to write a song for him. Paul wrote several songs, booked the musicians and Super Bear studio in Bene les Alpes, France, and Ringo agreed to record. The sessions were scheduled to begin July 11 and last through the 21st in 1980.

Alan Crowder, on behalf of Paul, called Lloyd Green and asked if he could play on a session Paul was producing on Ringo in France. Alan offered him the choice of flying first class on a regularly scheduled flight or to fly on the Concorde. Mindful of the cost of the Concord, Green chose the seven and a half hour flight to Paris instead of the much shorter Concorde and, later, thought he may have made a mistake.

The plane landed in Paris, then connected to a flight to Nice, where a limo picked Green up and drove about an hour and a half to Berre les Alpes, near Monaco, and up to the top of a mountain where the Super Bear Studios were located. Green stayed in a lodge about a half mile down the mountain from the studio.

Ringo had success recording the Carl Perkins' songs "Matchbox" and "Honey Don't" during his Beatles days so McCartney picked another Carl Perkins song, "Sure To Fall" that the Beatles had performed in Hamburg and at the Cavern with Paul singing lead. The song is a stone country mid-tempo song drenched with Lloyd Green's steel guitar and features a 16 bar steel guitar break by Green.

McCartney wrote two songs, "Private Property" and "Attention" for Ringo to record. Green did not play on "Attention" but played on "Private Property," where the singer tells the world that his lady is "private property" and there should be "no trespassing."

Ringo met actress Barbara Bach while both were filming *Caveman* and they fell in love. In the studio, Ringo talked about how much he loved Barbara and concluded with "you can't fight lighting." This led to a jam session with Ringo playing guitar (he can reportedly only play the major chords in the key of "A"--A, D and E) with Paul on drums, Laurence Juber on electric guitar and Lloyd Green playing dobro. They recorded the song with Linda

THE BEATLES AND COUNTRY MUSIC

McCartney and Sheila Casey, wife of saxophonist Howie Casey, on backing vocals. Barbara played maracas. Ringo loved the song so much that he wanted to name the album *Can't Fight Lightning*.

On his last full day at Super Bear, McCartney and the musicians started work on "Love's Full Glory," a song Linda had written. Paul said, "Let's try to get this done" but it was "late at night, maybe 12 o'clock when we started so at two or three in the morning" Green was exhausted and since he had an early morning flight told the group "I've got to get a few hours sleep." McCartney asked if Green could stay another week but the steel guitarist had recording sessions scheduled for Monday morning and, since it was Saturday, he needed to leave.

The song was unfinished but Green was scheduled to return to England for a tour in September and October so McCartney asked if he could finish the song sometime during the tour when he had a day off. Green replied, "Yes." [1]

Touring With Wings

Sitting by the pool with Laurence Juber on his second day in France, Green asked Juber what it was like to tour with Wings "and he started telling me all these wonderful things and I started getting a little envious," remembered Green. "He said that during a two month tour they leased an estate in Dallas, Texas and they had a 727 private jet. They flew from the estate to the show each night and then flew back to the estate. They had a round the clock English chef, French chef, had a doctor on call. He said that if you coughed someone would say 'let's get to the doctor.' It was like a self-contained village. I had not been on the road much since my early days with Faron Young, which were not like that at all. Juber said that when they got to the city where the show was, they'd walk down the ramp and there's security on both sides and they'd immediately get into a limo which took them to the venue where everything was set up. They'd go through a sound check, then food was brought in. Immediately after the show they were whisked into the limos and driven back to the airplane but they couldn't get on board because they had to stand on the side of the ramp and wait for Paul and Linda to get back. It might be an hour, hour and a half or two hours but they had to wait until Paul and Linda came back because all of this was being filmed. When Paul and Linda got out of their limo and walked up the ramp they waved at them. This happened every night."

Green told Jubar, "Well, that last part would not have appealed to me. I wouldn't have felt comfortable doing that."

Lloyd Green and Paul – the Last Session

Lloyd Green was booked on the Wembley Festival in 1976 by promoter Mervyn Conn. "It was a big success so he wanted me to do some tours for him and I did two 30 day tours, one in 1978 and one in 1980," said Green. "I didn't hear from Paul until the week before we left for the 1980 tour and he called me himself; Alan Crowder didn't call. Paul said 'I've got your schedule'— he knew my exact schedule—'and you've got one day off on September 25.'"

The tour consisted of the Glaser Brothers, Jimmy C. Newman, Billie Jo Spears and Lloyd Green, each performing for thirty minutes. "We stayed in London and a big bus drove us all over the U.K.," said Green. "Mervyn always flew my wife, Dot, with me so we had a great time.

During their phone call, McCartney told Green, "'I'll book the studio down in East Sussex' — it was about ten miles from where he lived — 'Would you come down and do this for me?' Green asked, "How will I get down" and McCartney replied "Somebody will pick you up."

Early on Thursday morning, September 25, "at six or seven o'clock, Alan Crowder pulled up in a limousine with a limo driver wearing the whole English bit," remember Green. On the way down, Green had the limo stop so he could purchase a watermelon because he knew Linda loved watermelons. "I think it was a three or four hour drive to get there," said Green, who gave Linda the watermelon and was warmly thanked. "We started recording as soon as we got there. He had the track of 'Love's Full Glory' going when we started around two o'clock that afternoon. By ten or eleven that night I'd already put about 12 tracks of steel guitar on the song. He had me playing the steel guitar in every direction and I was getting really really spacey and none of it was starting to make sense. He'd come out and say, 'Now I want you to do one like a bassoon.'"

Around ten or eleven that night, the McCartneys received a phone call telling them that John Bonham, the 32-year old drummer for Led Zeppelin, had died. "The moment he got that call everything died," said Green. "Total, complete silence. I don't know if he came out or Alan Crowder came out and said, 'The session's over. Paul can't work any more' and he told me what happened." [1]

Linda McCartney

Linda was very possessive and protective, "an extreme guardian of Paul's because women everywhere were—my God— they all wanted him so it was justifiable. But he loved her, he just adored her," said Green. Linda was known to be extremely jealous of other women but "Dot went with me to East Sussex and she couldn't have been more gracious, more warm and Dot's a beautiful woman," said Green, adding that "Paul was real gracious to her. He said, 'Dot, what a wonderful name. My first girlfriend was named Dot.'"

"I didn't charge them for that session because I felt it was an obligation because I hadn't finished it in France," said Green. "I told him, 'I don't want any money for this, Paul' and he said 'We've got to give you something.' He and Linda wanted me and Dot to spend the night on their estate but I said 'We can't do that because we're leaving at seven o'clock in the morning for the next date from London. I told them 'We'd love to but we just can't.' Linda said 'We can't let you leave without something' and she had fixed a wonderful meal. She was a great cook, a vegetarian and Dot and I are not strict vegetarians but 90 percent of our meals are vegetarian. Linda was an incredible cook."

Linda gave Lloyd and Dot "one of the first printings of a photographic book she had done. There have been a number of subsequent printings. She said she had four copies left out of a hundred so I got number 97 and she and Paul both wrote long inscriptions on the front page and signed it. She's was a real sweetheart."

The song "Love's Full Glory," with Linda singing lead, was posthumously released on the album, *Wide Prairie* by Linda McCartney on October 27, 1998; Linda McCartney died six months earlier, on April 17. [1]

Can't Fight Lightning: The Sessions

During his time in France, Ringo told Lloyd Green that John Lennon had finally agreed to be part of the album and they "were going to have dinner in New York to discuss the project." George Harrison had already agreed to produce some tracks for the album.

In August, Ringo recorded "You've Got a Nice Way," co-written and produced by Stephen Stills; Michael Stergis was the other co-writer. Ringo had drummed on Stills' debut solo album and Stills had played on Ringo's hit single, "It Don't Come Easy." This was followed by sessions with Rolling Stones' guitarist Ron Wood in September; one of their jam sessions led to the song "Dead Giveaway." Harry Nilsson produced a new version of "Back Off Boogaloo" as well as "Stop and Take the Time To Smell The Roses" and "Drumming Is My Madness."

In November, at George Harrison's studio in his home at Friar Park, Ringo recorded "Wrack My Brain," written by Harrison and the pop classic, "You Belong To Me," credited to country songwriters Pee Wee King and Redd Stewart with Chilton Price. Price, the music librarian at WAVE Radio in Louisville, wrote the song, originally titled "Hurry Home to Me" and King changed the lyric and melody slightly. In exchange for recording and promoting the song, Chilton gave King and Stewart songwriting credit. King and Stewart also wrote "The Tennessee Waltz," "Slow Poke" and "Bonaparte's Retreat."

"You Belong To Me" was originally recorded by country singer Sue Thompson in 1952, then covered by Patti Page. The biggest hit was by Jo Stafford, whose version reached number one on the *Billboard* pop chart in the Fall of 1952. Dean Martin also had a hit with the song, which was recorded by a number of singers, including Bing Crosby and Patsy Cline. George Harrison probably heard the song when it was released by Gene Vincent on his album *Gene Vincent Rocks and the Blue Caps Roll* in 1958.

Ringo recorded another Harrison-penned song, "All Those Years Ago," written for him but the vocal range was reportedly too high for Ringo and it was never released. After some revision, Harrison recorded the song and it was a hit for him in the summer of 1981.

The recording session with John Lennon never happened; he apparently planned to produce two songs he wrote, "Life Begins at 40" and "Nobody Told Me" for Ringo. Those plans, which would have meant that all four Beatles were on one album, ended on Monday night, December 8, 1980 when the 40-year old Lennon was assassinated outside his Dakota apartment in New York.

Good-bye, John

The last time Ken Mansfield saw John Lennon was on June 12, 1976. Ringo had invited Mansfield to his home in Beverly Hills so he could hear Waylon Jennings' new album *Are You Ready for the Country* that Mansfield produced. Ken walked into the living room and "was surprised to see John slouched moodily on the couch."

Lennon was in Los Angeles to play piano on a song he wrote, "Cookin' (In the Kitchen of Love)" for Ringo's album, *Rotogravure*. John was not friendly and Mansfield soon left, but he obtained Lennon's signature on a document that allowed the Beatle's song, "Hey Jude" to be recorded as "Hey Dude" by Jessi Colter, Waylon's wife and singer of the hit single, "I'm Not Lisa," produced by Mansfield.

"I had bribed Ringo for his signature with a private, exclusive playback of Waylon's album," said Mansfield, "I bribed Paul by sending him a pair of sunglasses from Rodeo Drive that he had seen in a fashion magazine. I took advantage of John's mood and bribed him by leaving Ringo's house." [1]

Norbert Putnam and George Harrison

Norbert Putnam and David Briggs are not "country" musicians, although they have recorded on a number of sessions for country artists. Their roots are in Muscle Shoals and the R&B music that came out of the studios there.

Putnam and Briggs opened Quad Studios in Nashville and Norbert produced "The Night They Drove Old Dixie Down" on Joan Baez (#3 on the pop chart in 1971). This led Putnam to produce Dan Fogleberg, Jimmy Buffett, Donovan, Brewer and Shipley and J.J. Cale.

George Harrison founded Dark Horse Records in 1971; the first signings were Ravi Shankar and Splinter, a two man group.

Splinter had initial success with their singles and an album produced by Harrison but "they didn't like working with George," said Putnam. "They thought everything they did sounded too much like the Beatles."

Dennis Morgan, General Manager at Dark Horse, wanted Putnam to meet with George Harrison to discuss producing Splinter. They met at Morgan's home in Los Angeles and George stated that he wanted Splinter's sessions done at his home studio in Friar's Park in England for tax reasons but Putnam could hire any musicians he chose. Putnam brought David Briggs and drummer Jerry Carrigan and they recorded the Splinter album, *Two Man Band,* which was released in 1977.

Later, Norbert, his wife and three other couples went to London during Christmas season in the late 1970s and Putnam called Harrison and left a message, inviting him down to London for drinks. Harrison called back and invited the group to Friar's Park at Henley-on-Thames. Putnam demurred; the people with him were not used to meeting celebrities and he thought it might be awkward. Harrison insisted they come, telling them to stay at the near-by Red Lion Hotel, have dinner and then come up to Frair's Park for drinks.

The group went up after dinner and Olivia, Harrison's wife, poured the drinks. Harrison "was very entertaining," remembered Putnam. "He was very engaged and entertained them. There are about 44 rooms in Friar's Park and George gave them a tour of seven or eight rooms then, after two hours, we went back to the hotel." Harrison had told Putnam that after the group was back at the hotel, he wanted to see him alone so Putnam went back.

Harrison told Putnam he wanted to play him three songs. "I'm thinking of hanging it up," said Harrison. "My last record only sold 300,000 in America. Honestly, I wonder if I still have it or if I've lost it."

"Have you played these for anyone else?" asked Putnam.

"Eric [Clapton] was up a short time ago," replied Harrison.

"He stared at me the whole time he played those tracks," remembered Putnam, who was enthused. "He played the best slide guitar. I told him 'You are one of the most unique artists in the world. Whenever I hear a record by you, I know it's you. I can't say the same about McCartney.'"

Harrison and Putnam opened some bottles of Bushnell's and they talked into the night. Putnam asked him, "Where do you keep your awards?" Harrison took him to a large bathroom, opened the door and there were gold records hanging on the walls. "I keep them in the shitter," said Harrison.

Harrison asked Putnam to "tell me everything about Elvis," adding "We met him in Los Angeles but we were nervous so we smoked dope in the car on the way over and when we got there we couldn't talk. He thought we were imbeciles."

Putnam had played on over a hundred recordings by Elvis but said, "I really don't know much about him. I played on his records but it was all in the studio." Putnam related that Elvis would listen to a demo, sing the song several times with the demo, ask "you guys got that?" (the musicians wrote their charts as they listened to the demo) and he was ready to record.

"Elvis had the microphone in his right hand and the lyrics in his left hand," said Putnam. "He was right in front of the drums but those drummers, like Jerry Carrigan, Kenny Buttrey and Buddy Harman, played much softer." During the 1960s, the session musicians did not use headphones; during the early Beatles records, the group did not use headphones either. It was not part of the recording process. There was no separate drum booth for drums so the drummer had to play softer because they were in the same room as the other musicians.

Norbert wanted to know about the Beatles.

"All the Beatles agreed that there wasn't anybody as strong as Presley," said Harrison. "He changed everything. He was fearless. All the Beatles knew that."

Harrison talked about Carl Perkins and admitted that "All of my early solos came from Carl Perkins." [1] After those initial recordings, Harrison developed his own style—but his guitar playing was rooted in Carl Perkins.

"I tried to build him up," said Putnam. "He was having doubts about himself and his music."

The Greens Back in Nashville

After Lloyd and Dot Green returned from the U.K. in October, "I received some gifts from Paul and Linda," said Green. "I wrote a few letters and he wrote some although Linda was the one who usually wrote the letters. They sent Dot and me Christmas cards every year from their estate either in Scotland or East Sussex. We just corresponded, but not significantly. However, after John Lennon was killed, I didn't hear from him again until I recorded 'I'm Looking Through You.'"

A Letter from Paul to Lloyd Green

In 1987 Lloyd Green contracted Menieres disease, an inner ear disorder and stopped doing sessions for 15 years. A specialist told him he would lose all of his hearing if he didn't get out of the studio and away from the headphones that musicians use when recording. Further, even after quitting, the specialist told Lloyd he would probably not survive with over fifty percent of his hearing during his lifetime.

At the age of 50, after 25 years and thousands of recording sessions, Green quit. "I had a good retirement, had plenty of money so it just seemed like a good opportunity," said Green. "I didn't listen to the radio or television real loud; everything was kept low volume. Then, in 1994, Green woke up and told his wife, "All that high pitched ringing is gone." Also gone was the dizziness that goes with Menieres.

Lloyd Green began playing again and touring; he is popular in Europe and he and Dot traveled around the world. In 2003, he decided to record an album, *Revisited*. Producer Russ Pahl, a big Beatles fan, suggested he record a Beatles song, "I'm Looking Through You," written primarily by McCartney.

"Russ and all the musicians on the session wanted me to send it to Paul but I didn't want to do that," said Green. "But they kept insisting so I finally sent the song and a letter that said something like 'I hope this captured the spirit of your song' and some things like that and sent it to Alan Crowder with McCartney's organization. Paul sent me a letter saying he loved the recording and he loved my steel playing. I told the musicians about it and they all wanted to see it so I gave a copy to Russ and all the musicians came by to read it. It was like I had received a letter from God because those session musicians are Beatles fans." [1]

Stop and Smell the Roses

The album *Can't Fight Lightning*, later renamed *Stop and Smell the Roses*, has a long and winding history. After the cover photo was taken at the Griffith Observatory in Los Angeles, where an electrical device made it appear that lightning bolts were coming out of Ringo's head, he wanted to change the name of the album to *Ringostein*. The executives at Portrait Records suggested *Starrdust*, which Ringo rejected.

The final mixes for the ten song album were delivered to Portrait in February but the executives at the label did not believe the album had commercial appeal and dropped Ringo from their roster in April. Starr then signed with Boardwalk, an indie label started by Neil Bogart, whose Casablanca label had been successful with disco.

Bogart decided to change the name of the album to *Stop and Smell the Roses* but other executives at the label, believing the album was not commercially viable, asked that "Can't Fight Lightning" and two other songs be dropped and replaced by "Sure To Fall," "Drumming Is My Madness" and the new, revised "Back Off Boogaloo." The vinyl album released contained the McCartney song "Private Property" but Green's steel guitar had been removed; however, "Sure To Fall" was added on side two. The album was released on October 27, 1981 but sank quickly. Later, a CD was released with Green's steel guitar restored to "Private Property."

Waylon and Ringo

Ken Mansfield began working with Waylon Jennings as a producer and eventually moved to Nashville for a period of time in the 1980s. Mansfield produced "We Had It All," the single off the *Honky Tonk Heroes* album in 1973; "Are You Ready For the Country" and the *Are You Ready for the Country* album in 1976-1977 (the album was named the top country album of 1977 by *Record World* magazine); "Amanda," a number one single and "It'll Be Her" both on the *Ramblin Man* album in 1979; and the Waylon and Willie duet "A Couple More Years."

During a tour, Waylon was scheduled to play the Roxy in Los Angeles so Ringo called Mansfield and let him know he'd be there and would host a party after in "On the Rox," the private club above the Rox's showroom, This room was for the elite of the elite in the music biz.

Ringo and some "glam rocker" friends from England came to the club for Waylon's show. After the show, the Waylon "outlaw" entourage went up to the Club where the British group was waiting. "It was a bizarre scene," remembered Mansfield. "Here was this bunch of cowboys with their beards, cowboy hats and boots, and suspicious looks all sitting at the tables on one side of the room, separated from Ringo's rock'n'roll pals by an almost perfect dividing line of tables down the center of the room. The English rock crew, with more of a glam look, was similarly ensconced on the other side of the room. Both sides were looking across this great cultural divide at each other in semi-bewilderment." [1]

"It was the funniest thing in the world," said Mansfield, "because when we got upstairs in the room all the cowboys got on one side of the room and Ringo and the rockers were on the other side of the room. So I walked to the middle of the room and Ringo walked out and Waylon came out and I introduced them to each other in the middle of the room. There was a brief pause and then everybody got together." [2]

Larry Hosford
& George Harrison

Larry Hosford was a singer-songwriter from Santa Cruz, California who landed an album deal with Shelter Records, owned by Leon Russell and Denny Cordell. Hosford's first album, *Lorenzo*, featured "Long Distance Kisses," which made the *Billboard* country chart. Hosford's sound was honky tonk hard core stone Okie country music. His second album, *Crosswords*, was produced by Dino Airali, who became president of George Harrison's Dark Horse record label, headquartered at the A&M Records office in Los Angeles.

Airali's assistant was Linda Arias, sister to Olivia Arias, who married George Harrison in 1978. Harrison had told Airali that he was open to studio work and Airali invited Leon Ruseell and Harrison to a session at Capitol Records Studio B for overdubs on Hosford's *Crosswords* album. On "Direct Me," Russell first added piano, then Harrison added a slide guitar. On "Wishing I Could," Harrison joined Russell and Hosford for backing vocals on the chorus.

It was a unique and thrilling experience for Hosford, but he never saw the former Beatle again. The *Crosswords* album was released in 1975, the same year as Harrison's *Extra Texture* album. [1]

New Moon Over Jamaica

During the 1987 Christmas holidays, Johnny Cash went to Jamaica, where he had a home on Cinnamon Hill, and Paul McCartney and his family came by.

"Tom T. and Dixie Hall were there," remembered John Carter Cash, "and I had a friend with me, who was the drummer in my rock band. Paul and Linda came over—they were a little late—with Stella, Mary and their son—he had red-hair—James. They were vegans; Linda said she never ate anything with a heart, so we had a vegan meal."

After dinner, we went into the living room, talking, and Paul said, 'Why don't I go out and get my guitar.' My drummer was sitting on the porch by himself, just beating out a rhythm with some pencils, and Paul came to the porch and just started jamming with him, just having fun, playing music. He was out there for awhile and finally my Mom said, 'Where's Paul?' He was out there just having fun and jamming."

"Paul was just so kind and outgoing," continued Cash. "He made you feel like you were the only person in a room."

Tom T. had the inspiration for "New Moon Over Jamaica," and he and Cash began writing it with Paul "offering a few lines here and there," said Cash. "After it was finished, Paul wrote on the piece of paper 'I had absolutely nothing to do with this song.' Then my Dad wrote the same thing and Tom T. wrote the same thing. It was just a joke, really." The song had taken about 20-30 minutes to write. "We were all just sitting around, all of us when they wrote that," said Cash.

McCartney recorded the song in England "with a reggae feel," remembered Cash. "Then they got together in England and recorded the version that's on the record." That recording was made on April 1, 1988 in McCartney's studio in London. The tape was then sent to Jack Clement in Nashville and he "added some things" and it was released on Cash's album *Water From the Wells of Home*, released on Mercury in May, 1988. On the song, which is in three-quarter waltz time, Paul and Linda McCartney, Tom T. Hall and June Carter sing harmony while Paul solos on part of a verse.

The album featured Cash doing duets with the Everly Brothers, Roy Acuff, Rosanne Cash, Emmylou Harris, Roy Acuff, Tom T. Hall, Hank Williams, Jr., Waylon Jennings, Glen Campbell, June Carter, John Carter Cash—and Paul McCartney.

"Paul had such charisma and magic," said Cash. "But he was so down to earth and made you feel special. Eric Clapton is like that too and so was my Dad. I met a lot of people through my Dad and I found that people like Paul McCartney, Billy Graham and Bill Clinton—there's a reason they are who they are. It's because of the way they're made. They have a magic that is very rare. It's like one in ten billion or something." [1]

Ringo and Dolly Parton

Ringo "was very intrigued by Dolly's career and had once stated to me that he would love to meet her," said Ken Mansfield. "Coincidentally, Dolly was a giant Beatles fan and, knowing that I had worked with them, had jokingly mentioned that someday she would like to meet them, Ringo in particular."

One night, when Ringo and Dolly were both in Los Angeles, Ken Mansfield arranged to have them both over for dinner—but did not tell either that the other was coming. "Both invitees were thrilled at the surprise," remembered Mansfield, "and the intimacy of the evening really made the whole thing very special." [1]

Dolly came by cab and Ringo, with his girlfriend at the time, Nancy Andrews, drove. The evening was filled with conversation and laughter as, once again, a Beatle connected with country music.

Act Naturally Redux

In 1989, Ringo recorded "Act Naturally" with Buck Owens at the Abbey Road Studio in London. Owens had left Capitol, where he had his string of hits, but in 1988 Jim Foglesong, head of Capitol's Nashville office, persuaded Buck to re-sign with the label. Capitol wanted to revive Buck's career and encouraged him to perform at the Wembley Festival in London, an annual event organized by concert promoter Mervyn Conn. [1] During the early 1960s Conn owned a club, Romano's on Gerrard Street in London and, with agent Joe Collins, had promoted the Beatles first Christmas show in 1963. Through Conn, Owens arranged to record a duet with Ringo during the time that Buck was in England during an international tour.

Owens stated that he spoke with Ringo on the phone, who agreed to do a duet of "Act Naturally." Waiting for Ringo at the studio, Owen expected "a big entourage—or at least an assistant or two. But he just came walking in by himself, said 'Hi' to everybody, and we went to work. During the session "me and Ringo just sang. I didn't play guitar and he didn't play drums. We let the Buckaroos just do their thing." [2]

The single and video were released in June. "Ringo told me he'd always been a big country music fan, so he was happy to have his first single to hit the country charts," said Owens. The duet reached number 27 on *Billboard's* country chart in 1989 and was nominated for a Country Music Association Award for "Vocal Event of the Year" but lost to Hank Williams and Hank Jr.'s recording of "There's a Tear in My Beer."

Old Friends

In 1996 the Carl Perkins tribute album, *Go Cat Go* was released and featured performances by all four former Beatles, although John Lennon's slot was him performing "Blue Suede Shoes" on his 1969 album *Live Peace from Toronto*. (The album also contained The Jimi Hendrix Experience performing "Blue Suede Shoes" from the Hendrix archive.)

On the album, which featured Perkins performing with John Fogerty, Tom Petty and the Heartbreakers, Paul Simon, Bono, Willie Nelson and Johnny Cash, he wrote a song with George Harrison, "Distance Makes No Difference With Love" that he recorded with Harrison playing guitar and singing harmony.

In 1981, during the time Paul McCartney was in Montserrat recording his *Tug of War* album, he called Carl Perkins to join him on a song, "Get It," that McCartney had written. Perkins spent eight days with McCartney and his family and on the night before he left, the song "My Old Friend" came to him. The song was about their friendship and has the line "think of me every now and then, my old friend," which reportedly is what Lennon said to McCartney the last time they visited—his parting words. The song was quite emotional for McCartney, who sang harmony on Perkins' cut on the *Go Cat Go* album.

Ringo Thirty-eight Years Later

On July 6, 2008, Ringo played the Wildhorse Saloon in Nashville with his tenth All-Starr Band. Before the concert, Tim Ghianna interviewed him for the *Nashville Scene* by phone. Starr was on the Canadian side of Niagara Falls when he spoke to the reporter about the *Beaucoups of Blues* sessions; Ghianna also interviewed some of the musicians on the session.

According to Charlie Daniels, who played guitar on the session, "It was remarkable that Starr left the rock pretense back on Abbey Road when he settled in at Music City Recorders on 19th Avenue." It was, Daniels said, "a pretty typical Nashville session. You know, three songs in three hours. It was go in, sit down and work. Here's the songs, here's the chords, let's get it done. It was not a Beatles-type leisurely session. It was work."

Drummer D.J. Fontana, who was Elvis Presley's drummer during the height of the rock star's career, admitted that the musicians "were looking forward to the paychecks, but not necessarily to working with a rock superstar." Fontana, who was 76 at the time of the interview, said "We were thinking he was going to be a jerk. I mean, The Beatles, the No. 1 act in the world. This guy's got all these big monster records. But he came here and it was, 'Whatever you guys want to do, let's do it. You guys play the way you've been playing and I'll try to catch up.'"

Talking about the recording sessions, Starr said, "We'd find five songs in the morning and then we'd record five songs at night."

"It all came together because I sent my car to pick up Pete Drake at the airport when he came in to record with George," Starr said. "He noticed I had a lot of country music in my car. Everyone always knew I liked country music." After the ride to the studio, Ringo and Drake met and were talking when Drake suggested, "Why don't you come down to Nashville and record an album?" He did and "it was fast and it was good," remembered Starr. "We did the whole thing in two days."

Engineer Scotty Moore, Elvis's guitar player, was the engineer and remembered that "There were too many people in the studio, in the control room and in the front row. It was so crowded you just couldn't breathe. But the session went fine."

"The sessions went until at least 1 a.m.," continued Moore. "But it was 2 or 3 in the morning before we got out of there. It took that long just to say goodnight to everybody," before adding, "For me it was a job, but I enjoyed meeting him and it was a good camaraderie."

Ringo stated that working with Moore "was an incredible experience [because] Scotty played all those guitar parts with Elvis."

D.J. Fontana remembered that "he's one of the finest drummers. People say 'He don't do a lot.' Well, he don't have to do a lot. He played that steady tempo. He was the glue for the Beatles. He put it together for them. That's what they needed. That's the whole secret of drumming. If you wanna do something fancy, go ahead and do it. If not, just play the beat."

During the jam session at the end of recording their songs for the album, Ringo got on the drums, laid down a beat and the musicians followed. "Ringo did it all," said Fontana. "I think one of the jams was 18 minutes. What amazed me, he never varied from that tempo. He had the greatest conception of tempo I've ever heard in my life. I have never heard anybody play that steady in my life, and that's a long time."

Although Fontana played drums on the session, for the jam he played "tambourine, claves, maracas. We were just picking up anything. When I tired of playing one, I'd pick up another. It went on and on as we went around the horn, everyone playing."

Charlie McCoy, who played organ, vibes and harmonica on the session said of the jam, "At the end of everything, after we had finished up the recording, Ringo went behind the drums and played and everybody jumped in. We just jumped in the groove. He played much better than I had the impression he played from just hearing The Beatles' records." McCoy added, "It was great working with him."

Discussing the reception of the *Beaucoups of Blues* album, Charlie Daniels said, "In retrospect, I don't think it was the explosive album [Apple executives] wanted it to be. I'm sure they wanted it to be a multi-million seller. But it was not in the Beatles tradition, like what George and the other guys had done" but it helped "legitimize country music in the rock world." [1]

Ringo At The Ryman

On July 7, 2013, Ringo Starr celebrated his 72nd birthday with a concert at the Ryman Auditorium in Nashville. In Ringo's "All Starr Band" were Steve Lukather (formerly of Toto), Richard Page (of Mr. Mister), Mark Rivera (formerly with Billy Joel), Gregg Rolie (formerly with Journey and Santana), Todd Rundgren and Gregg Bissonette. Ringo played drums and sang.

Ringo kicked off the concert with the Carl Perkins classic, "Matchbox," then sang "It Don't Come Easy" and "Wings" before Todd Rundgren did the Hank Williams classic, "I Saw the Light."

Gregg Rolie did a song from his Santana days, "Evil Ways" while Steve Lukather brought back "Rosanna" from his days with Toto. Richard Page followed with "Kyrie Eleison," a hit from Mr. Mister.

Ringo came back to the vocal mike and did "Don't Pass Me By," a song he wrote for the Beatles, then Todd Rundgren did "Bang the Drum All Day" before Ringo did "Boys" and "Yellow Submarine" from his Beatle days. Gregg Rolie did another Santana song ("Black Magic Woman") before the band and crowd launched into "Happy Birthday" for Ringo.

Following this, Ringo sang "Anthem" and John Lennon's song, "I'm the Greatest" before special guest Joe Walsh—and a former member of Ringo's "All Starr Band"—performed "Rocky Mountain Way" followed by Richard Page doing "You Are Mine." One of Toto's biggest hits, "Africa," was sung by Steve Lukather, then Gregg Rolie sang "Everybody's Everything."

Ringo took over vocals again with the Beatles' "I Wanna Be Your Man," then Todd Rundgren did "Love Is The Answer," Richard Page did "Broken Wings" and Steve Lukather did "Hold the Line."

The concert ended with three songs from Ringo: "Photograph," "Act Naturally" and "With a Little Help From My Friends," that segued into "Give Peace a Chance."

On "With a Little Help From My Friends," Ringo was joined by Nashville country stars Brad Paisley, Vince Gill, Kix Brooks, songwriter Gary Burr, Brendan Benson and former All Starr Band alums Richard Marx and Felix Cavaliere.

Paul and Buddy Holly

Paul McCartney never lost his love for Buddy Holly's music. McCartney purchased the Buddy Holly publishing catalogue in 1971 and now owns the songs Holly wrote, such as "That'll Be The Day" (the first song that Lennon and McCartney learned and the first song they recorded back in their early Liverpool days). In 1976 McCartney initiated a "Buddy Holly Week" and performed regularly during the Buddy Holly Tribute Concert. During the 1976 show, McCartney received the cuff links Holly was wearing on his last flight from Holly's former producer, Norman Petty. In 1985 McCartney hosted a video documentary on Holly. In June, 2011 McCartney appeared on the Tribute to Buddy Holly album, *Rave On* singing "It's So Easy" and, during his 2014 tour, requested a date for Lubbock, Texas, Holly's home town where a statue of the singer appears outside the main arena. That date had to be postponed from June to October, but when he played Lubbock, McCartney performed Buddy Holly's "It's So Easy" during his show.

Nashville on Tour 2014

During his 2014 tour, McCartney performed in Nashville on October 16. McCartney performed 30 songs over almost three hours. He started about an hour late; the concert was scheduled to begin at 8 p.m. but did not start until 8:58.

Prior to the concert there was a double scroll—one on each side of the stage—comprised of clips from McCartney's life. The songs from the Beatles and McCartney after the Beatles used the original recordings with strong disco/Latin drums inserted. Backstage, special guests waited in a "Green Room" before they were ushered in to meet McCartney. Ernie Winfrey was among the guests; "There were a bunch of people making sure I got there," said Winfrey. "When I was with him I said, 'I don't know if you remember me' but McCartney quickly said, 'Yes, you're Ernie.'" Winfrey had several pictures from the 1970s that he gave him and McCartney thanked him. It was a short talk; a brief chat.

On the deluxe *Venus and Mars* album, McCartney remastered the songs and added a number of songs and pictures from Nashville and gave Ernie Winfrey credit for mixing "Hey Diddle."

Also back stage were Reba McEntire, Ronnie Dunn and Alice Cooper.

McCartney's concert entrance was simple: he strolled on the stage, wearing black slacks, a white shirt with a black collar and a black stripe down the front and a dark blue sports coat, leading five musicians.

McCartney began the concert playing his Hofner bass and sang "The Magical Mystery Tour," "Save Us" and then said, "Great to be back here. We love this place!" before he launched into "All My Loving." The 20,000 fans in attendance gave him loud applause while McCartney stood on stage, soaking it in. "This is so cool," he said. "I've just got to take a minute and drink it in. This is for myself." After that moment he sang "Listen To What the Man Said" and, when he finished, took off his bass and sports coat. "This will be the only wardrobe change," he said before he strapped on a Les Paul Gibson and sang "Let Me Roll It," followed by a short jam on Jimi Hendrix's "Purple Haze."

"We released *Sergeant Pepper* on a Friday and on Sunday we went to see Jimi Hendrix play," said McCartney, "and he had learned it. He played it crazy wild. At the end his guitar was out of tune and he said, 'Is Eric here?' He was looking for Eric Clapton to tune his guitar. Eric was sliding down in his seat, hiding away. That jam was a tribute to Hendrix."

McCartney put on an Epiphone electric and said "This was the guitar I played on the original recording of this song" before he launched into "Paperback Writer." McCartney took off his guitar, went to the piano in the back of the stage and said, "This is for Nancy—who is here tonight. This is for you, Nance" and played "My Valentine."

McCartney asked the audience, "Anybody here a Wings fan?" and the audience cheered, then he sang "Nineteen Hundred and Eighty Five" followed by "The Long and Winding Road" with a backdrop showing scenes from Liverpool. Still at the piano, he played "Maybe I'm Amazed" after saying "I wrote this for Linda." Leaving the piano McCartney put on a Martin acoustic guitar and sang "I've Just Seen a Face" then, after the applause said "Thank you, Nashville." "We Can Work It Out" was next, followed by "Another Day."

"I have great memories of Nashville," said McCartney, "we recorded some here" as he gave a shout-out to Ernie Winfrey and pointed to him in the audience. "We've got to save the studios here," he said. Most of those in the audience thought it was a reference to the fact that RCA Studio A, where numerous acts had recorded, was set to be destroyed by a developer who planned on constructing condos. (The studio was later "saved" when Aubrey Preston, Mike Curb and Chuck Elcen purchased it from the developer.) However, McCartney was actually referring to the studio on Division Street where he had recorded in 1974; that studio had been sold and was set to be demolished so condos would be constructed on that site.

Playing his Martin, he did "And I Love Her" and then "Blackbird," alone on stage as the stage rose as he played.

Sitting at a colorful electric piano, McCartney performed "New," "Queenie" and "Lady Madonna." "This is from "Yellow Submarine" he said to introduce "All Together Now." He played a 12-string sunburst acoustic and said "This is from *Sergeant Pepper*" before playing "Lovely Rita" then did "Everybody Out There" before he returned to his Martin and sang "Eleanor Rigby," which started with McCartney playing alone while his musicians sang harmony.

He returned to his Hofner bass, said "This is from the *Sergeant Pepper's* album" and played "For the Benefit of Mr. Kite."

Picking up a ukulele, McCartney talked about George Harrison while pictures of Harrison were on the backdrop. "George was a great ukulele player before it became popular," he said. "I went over to George's house one day and told him 'I've learned one of your songs on the ukulele. 'Something.'" McCartney started "Something" alone with the uke, but the song became a full production as he sang it.

As he put on his Hofner bass he told the audience they "need to sing" then launched into "Ob-la-di-ob-la–da" followed by

"Band on the Run" and "Back in the U.S.S.R." While he moved to the piano he told the audience he'd wanted to play Russia "and finally got invited. It was lovely" then related how he met "all these government ministers backstage and the Defense Minister told him 'First record I bought, 'Love Me Do.' Another minister said 'I learned how to speak English from Beatles songs. 'Hello Goodbye.'" McCartney swore those stories were true.

McCartney sang "Let It Be" as the audience sang along, followed by "Live and Let Die," which was accompanied by loud explosions and fireworks.

Back to the electric piano he sang "Hey Jude" as the audience once again sang along and then he walked off the stage.

McCartney returned to the stage for his encore waving a large American flag, followed by his musicians carrying Tennessee and British flags. He put on his Hofner bass and sang "Day Tripper," "Birthday," and "I Saw Her Standing There" before, once again, he left the stage.

For his second encore, McCartney came out alone with his right-handed Epiphone acoustic guitar strung for a left hander and sang "Yesterday" before he was joined by his band and did "Helter Skelter." He finished the evening at the piano doing an Abbey Road medley beginning with "Golden Slumbers," and "Carry That Weight," switching to his Les Paul Gibson during the song.

That was the end of the concert. It was 11:38 p.m.

Beatles Songs in Country Music

The country song that connects the Beatles with country music best is "Bigger Than the Beatles" by Joe Diffie, which was on the *Billboard* country chart 1995-1996 and rose to number one, a position it held for two weeks. The song was not a "Beatles" song but the singer compares his love for his girl to the Beatles and says his love is "bigger" than the legendary group. In terms of success on country radio and the *Billboard* country chart, the biggest Beatles song is "I Don't Want to Spoil the Party" by Rosanne Cash, which was a number one country hit in 1989. The next best showing on the *Billboard* country chart of a Beatles song is "I Feel Fine" by the Sweethearts of the Rodeo, which reached number nine in 1989.

During the Beatles' recording of "I Feel Fine," John Lennon stated "George and I play the same bit on guitar together—that's the bit that'll set your feet a-tapping, as the reviews say. I suppose it has a bit of a country-and-western feel about it, but then so have a lot of our songs." [1]

Other Beatle songs on the *Billboard* country chart were "All My Lovin'" by Mundo Earwood (#58 in 1982); "I've Just Seen a Face" by Calamity Jane (Pam Rose, Mary Fielder, Linda Moore and Mary Ann Kennedy; #44 in 1982). "Yesterday" by Billie Jo Spears (#60 in 1979) and "Get Back" by Steve Wariner (#72, 1995).

In 1995, Liberty Records released an album: *Come Together: America Salutes the Beatles*. On that album were "I'll Follow the Sun" by David Ball, "Something" by Tanya Tucker, "One After 909" by Willie Nelson, "The Long and Winding Road" by John Berry, "Come Together" by Delbert McClinton, "If I Fell" by

Sammy Kershaw, "Let It Be" by Collin Raye, "We Can Work It Out" by Phil Keaggy and PFR, "Yesterday" by Billy Dean, "Can't Buy Me Love" by Shenandoah, "Nowhere Man" by Randy Travis, "Oh! Darling" by Huey Lewis, "Help" by Little Texas, "In My Life" by Susan Ashton and Gary Chapman, "Get Back" by Steve Wariner, "All My Loving" by Suzy Bogguss and Chet Atkins and "Paperback Writer" by Kris Kristofferson.

In 2005, the label American Beat released *Yesterday: Country Music Tribute to the Beatles*. On that album were "Eight Days a Week" by Lorrie Morgan, "Something" by Willie Nelson, "You've Got to Hide Your Love Away" by Waylon Jennings, "Yesterday" by Willie Nelson and Merle Haggard, "I Don't Want to Spoil the Party" and "I'm Only Sleeping" by Rosanne Cash, "I Feel Fine" by the Sweethearts of the Rodeo, "Help" by Dolly Parton, "Let It Be" by John Denver, "Blackbird" by Collin Raye, "Fool on the Hill" by Ray Stevens and "Michelle" by Chet Atkins.

In 2013 Reviver Records released *Let Us In Americana: The Music of Paul McCartney*. On that album were "Come and Get It" by the Wood Brothers, "Yellow Submarine" by Buddy Miller, "Band on the Run" by Will Hoge, "I'm Looking Through You" by Jim Lauderdale, "My Love" by Holly Williams, "Let Me Roll It" by Teddy Thompson, "Fool on the Hill" by Bruce Cockburn, "Get Back" by Ollabelle, "Let 'Em In" by Lee Ann Womack, "I Will" by Steve Earle, featuring Allison Moorer, "Every Night" by Rodney Crowell, "Yesterday" by Matraca Berg, "Give Ireland Back to the Irish" by Ketch Secor, "I've Just Seen a Face" by Sam Bush, "Uncle Albert/Admiral Halsey" by Ed Snodderly and "Let It Be" by The McCrary Sisters.

"I've Just Seen a Face" has been recorded by Pure Prairie League, Billy Burnette (son of Dorsey Burnette), The Dillards, and the Forester Sisters. "I'm Looking Through You" and "One After 909" were recorded by Steve Earle. "Let It Be" was recorded by John Denver and Gary & Randy Scruggs and "Norwegian Wood" was recorded by Waylon Jennings. On Emmylou Harris' first album, *Pieces of the Sky*, she recorded "Here, There and Everywhere."

Bluegrass has been most open to Beatles songs. An album, *Bluegrass Beatles* by Craig Duncan, was comprised of "Love Me Do," "Ticket to Ride," "Can't Buy Me Love," "All My Lovin'," "Here There and Everywhere," "We Can Work It Out," "If I Fell," "I Want to Hold Your Hand," "I Will," "Eleanor Rigby," "And I Love Her," "Yesterday" and "Hey Jude."

On *Pickin' On the Beatles: A Bluegrass Tribute*, the two disc CD set contained "Strawberry Fields Forever," "And I Love Her," "Ticket to Ride," "Norwegian Wood," "I Want to Hold Your Hand," "Paperback Writer," "Can't Buy Me Love," "Hey Jude," "She Loves You," "Yellow Submarine," "Hard Day's Night," "Eleanor Rigby," "Eight Days a Week," "Get Back," "Blackbird," "With a Little Help From My Friends," "Hello, Goodbye," "If I Fell," "Help," "Love Me Do," "Penny Lane," "We Can Work It Out" and "Let It Be."

The Del McCoury Band recorded "When I'm 64" on their *Moneyland* album and "Eleanor Rigby" was recorded by Sam Bush and Alan Munde on their *Together For the First Time* album. Alison Krauss recorded "I Will" on her 1995 album *Now That I've Found You: A Collection*.

Other bluegrass renditions of Beatles songs are: "Blackbird" by The Jaybirds, "Norwegian Wood" by Tim O'Brien, "One

After 909" by Belle Monroe, "The Night Before" by Larry Rice, "I'm Down" by the New Grass Revival on their *Friday Night in America* album, "Because" by Mike Marshal, "You've Got to Hide Your Love Away" by 2nd Generation, "Yesterday" by Bobby Clark, "Don't Let Me Down" by The Dillards, "Two of Us" by John Reischman on Butch Baldassari's Tribute album *The Road Home* and "I've Just Seen a Face" by New Tradition.

The Charles River Valley Boys did an album, *Beatles Country,* that contained "I've Just Seen a Face," "Baby's in Black," "I Feel Fine," "Yellow Submarine," "Ticket to Ride," "And Your Bird Can Sing," "What Goes On," "Norwegian Wood," "Paperback Writer," "She's a Woman," "I Saw Her Standing There" and "Help."

The Grassmasters are a bluegrass group that performs Beatles songs. On their album, *Beatles Grass,* they recorded "We Can Work it Out," "Dr. Robert," "I'm Looking Through You," "Things We Said Today," "Can't Buy Me Love," "Hard Days Night," "Act Naturally," "Do You Want to Know a Secret," "What Goes On," "Another Girl," "I've Just Seen a Face" and "Yesterday."

Country Songs

Country Music was described by Country Music Hall of Fame songwriter Harlan Howard as "three chords and the truth." There are still three chord songs in country music, but that is increasingly rare. The influence of the Beatles songs on contemporary country music is often found in the bridge of "middle eight" as they called it. While most country songs before the Beatles generally had four chords—the 1-4-5 in a chord progression with the 2 an "off chord," a number of country songs may go to a 3 and 6 in the chord pattern for the bridge. For example, let's say a song is in "C." In the "standard" country song it would start in "C" then go to "F" or "G7" in a pattern. For the bridge, the song might go from the "C" to a "D7"—or to an "F" then a "D7" before it resolved on "G."

A Beatles song often went from "C" to "E minor" then "A minor," then possibly a "D minor" or "D minor 7" before it resolved to "G." For the verse, a Beatles song may have gone from "C" to "A minor" or "C" to "E minor" then "F." Songs vary but adding the "E minor," "A minor" and "D minor 7" into the bridge of a song in "C" is something first found in Beatles songs before it became an accepted part of country music songs.

Epilogue

The Beatles had deep roots in country music because Liverpool, where they grew up, has deep roots in country music. Some of the first songs they heard and played were "country" or "folk" songs, called "skiffle" in England. The earliest rock'n'roll was rockabilly, coming primarily out of Sun Studios in Memphis. That early rock'n'roll was deeply rooted in country music and this is the music the Beatles cut their teeth on. Those early influences— and early songs—stayed with them their entire lives. Elvis, Carl Perkins, Buddy Holly, Jerry Lee Lewis, the Everly Brothers –these were their first musical heroes and the Beatles began as a band covering the hits of these artists.

Country music has not traditionally been a music for young people; it has never been "cool" with a young crowd, especially after the rhythm and blues influence on rock and roll took hold. The world of country music has been traditional and conservative in a social and cultural sense while young people tend to be less bound by the past, more adventuresome, tolerant, open minded and intrigued by the wilder side of life. For most young people, rock and roll provides the soundtrack to their lives because it is a music of rebellion, and rebellion is part of growing up.

As noted in this book, Paul McCartney admitted to steel guitar player Lloyd Green that during his Beatle days and after he always liked country music but it "wasn't cool" to admit that.

Drummer Ringo Starr was the only Beatle to publicly acknowledge a love of country music. In an interview in *Melody Maker* in 1964, Ringo stated, "Ninety percent of the music I like is coloured" but admitted that for the remaining ten percent he "'really enjoyed good country and western,' being particularly fond of Buck Owens and Roger Miller." [1]

After the initial thrill of rockabilly, the Beatles, like many other British and American youths, became aware of the music of African-Americans. They had known and loved Chuck Berry and Little Richard—and done their songs—but those two artists could also be considered "rockabilly," albeit a wild and wooly rockabilly. Interestingly, many of the early R&B acts grew up hearing country music for a simple reason: country music was readily available on the radio, particularly the Saturday night "barn dances" such as the Grand Ole Opry, while the music of African-Americans was not heard much on radio until the early 1950s.

It was Motown and the commercial sound of Rhythm and Blues that excited the Beatles during their early recording career. Paul McCartney admitted that they felt "'Love Me Do' was us trying to do the blues. It came out whiter because it always does. We're white and we were just young Liverpool musicians. We didn't have any finesse to be able to actually sound black." McCartney continued, "If the Beatles ever wanted a sound it was R&B. That's what we used to listen to, what we used to like and what we wanted to be like. Black, that was basically it. Arthur Alexander." [2]

If you dig a bit deeper into what McCartney said, you will find the essence of the Beatles sound and what made them so unique. They had deep roots in country and rockabilly music, but after they heard R&B, they wanted to be "black." However, they could never be "black." Their background and their "whiteness" would not allow them to play "black music" convincingly in a soulful manner. In this, they were like Elvis—a country guy who loved and sang songs from African Americans, but could never be "totally black." This made it perfect for the white, mainstream audience who like African-American music—but at a safe distance.

Another thing that made The Beatles unique—and this has been somewhat overlooked—is their search for obscure "B" sides of singles to perform. Other bands did the top hits— that's what a cover band does—and the Beatles, a 1950s cover band, certainly did their share of hits, but they also sought out songs that were not hits. That gave them an edge, made them different, demonstrated they were adventurous and provided audiences with songs they had not heard. The Beatles played both sides of Carl Perkins' records, album cuts of Elvis, and "B" sides of R&B and pop hits.

One of those "B" sides was "Soldier of Love (Lay Down Your Arms)" that was the flip side of Arthur Alexander's single

"Where Have You Been (All My Life)." "Soldier of Love" was written by Buzz Cason and Tony Moon in Nashville. Cason had been a member of The Casuals, who were Brenda Lee's backing band and had solo success as Garry Miles; his single "Look For a Star" reched number 16 on *Billboard's* Hot 100 chart in 1960. Cason also co-wrote (with Mac Gayden) "Everlasting Love" which was recorded first by Robert Knight and then U2 and others as well as country hits for Martina McBride ("Love's the Only House"), The Derailers ("Cold Beer, Hot Love and Cool Country Music"), Tommy Overstreet, T.G. Sheppard, Mel Tillis, Alan Jackson, Freddy Weller and The Oaks. Cason built Creative Workshop studio in Nashville where artists such as Dolly Parton, Jerry Reed, the Judds and Emmylou Harris have recorded. [3]

"That's where we got our repertoire from, the B-sides, and 'Shot of Rhythm and Blues,' the lesser known stuff that we happened to bring to the fore, the R&B stuff," said McCartney. "Because it was just Cliff [Richard} before that. I certainly wanted to be like Elvis. We admired very much all the black recording artists and could hear how basic all their recordings were. And Buddy Holly's three chords." [4]

Rock and roll had pretty much left its wildest days behind around 1960, when Elvis got out of the Army. By this time, Elvis was no longer a musical leader; from this point forward in his career he followed the example of Bing Crosby, who recorded a wide variety of songs—pop, country, Hawaiian, Irish—to reach a wide audience. By 1960, rock and roll had been tamed; it was pretty white boys singing songs that came out of the African-American culture with the blackness diluted to a shade of light grey. Beatles producer George Martin stated that, in England prior to the Beatles, "the rock-and-roll gyrations of Tommy Steele and Cliff Richard were clinical, anaemic, even anaesthetic." [5]

When Elvis came along, he put a dose of African-American rhythm into country music; when the Beatles came along, they put a dose of country music into black music. No one has ever pointed that out for a simple reason; during the 1960s country music represented the polar opposite of rock and roll. Rock was liberal; country was conservative. Rock was for the young; country music was for the old. Rock was hip, cool and the counterculture. Country was down home, safe, law-abiding counter to the counterculture. Rock was long hair and blue jeans worn every day; country music was short hair and clothes other than blue jeans because that represented the look of rural farmers.

Country music was described by one writer of a Beatles biography as "the squarest, most right-wing genre in pop." [6] That was generally the consensus of Beatles fans during the 1960s and, for some, even today.

A book titled *The Beatles and Country Music* will no doubt draw serious head scratching from current as well as long-time Beatles fans. It shouldn't. Country music is as important to the history of rock and roll as rhythm and blues, although most rock historians have not embraced that idea. Country music is an integral part of the history of rock and, specifically, an integral part of the history of the Beatles.

At the Sound Shop recording studio are, standing, Paul McCartney, Buddy Killen and Tony Dorsey; seated are Ernie Winfrey and Linda McCartney. (Photo courtesy of Ernie Winfrey)

Engineer Ernie Winfrey and Paul McCartney during the Nashville recording sessions. (Photo courtesy of Ernie Winfrey)

Ernie Winfrey at the studio control board in Sound Shop during the time of the Nashville recording sessions of Paul McCartney and Wings. (Photo courtesy of Ernie Winfrey)

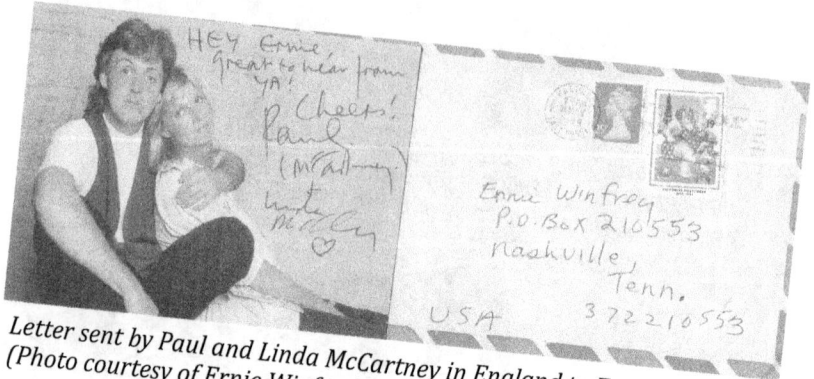

Letter sent by Paul and Linda McCartney in England to Ernie Winfrey. (Photo courtesy of Ernie Winfrey)

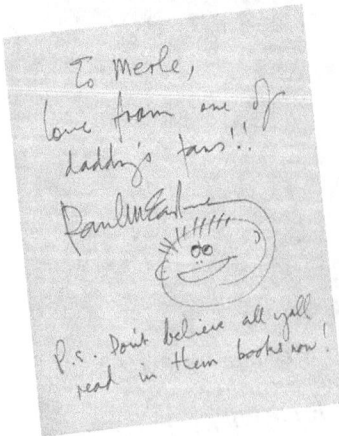

Merle Atkins Russell was reading "The Beatles: The Authorized Biography" by Hunter Davies when Paul McCartney visited with Chet Atkins at his home in Nashville. Paul signed this to Merle on the inside of the book. (Photo courtesy of Merle Russell)

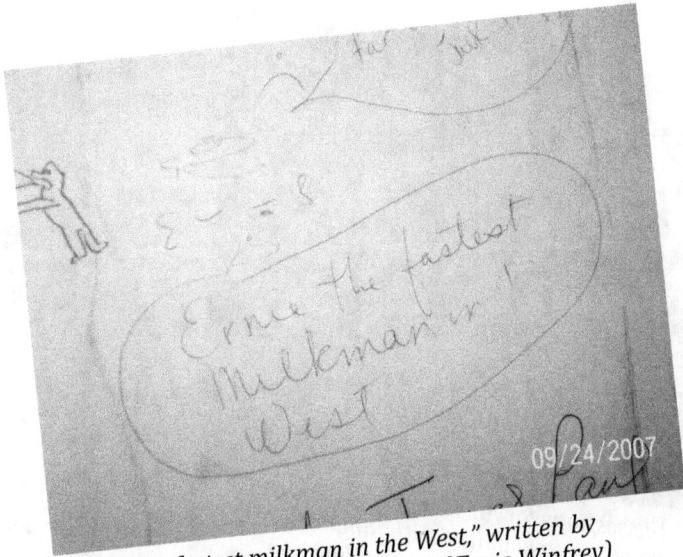

"Ernie the fastest milkman in the West," written by Linda McCartney. (Photo courtesy of Ernie Winfrey)

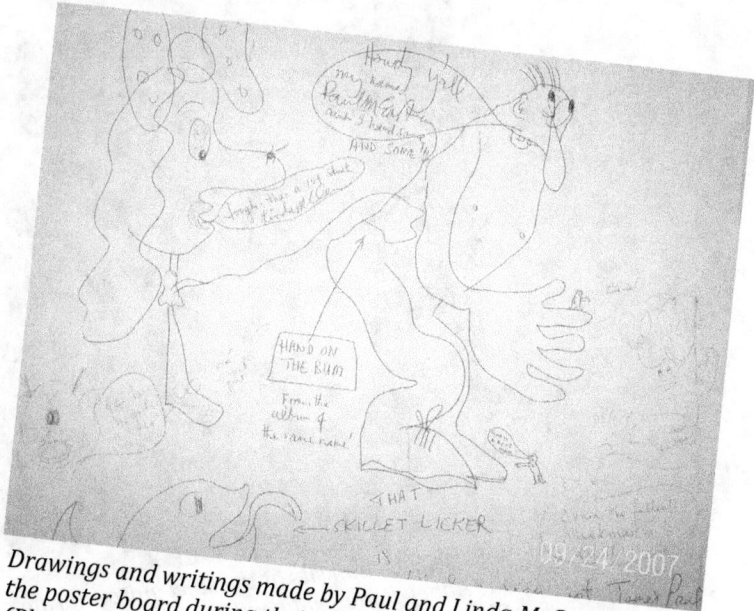

Drawings and writings made by Paul and Linda McCartney on the poster board during their visit to the Sound Shop studio. (Photo courtesy of Ernie Winfrey)

During the sessions for All Things Must Pass, Pete Drake sits at the steel guitar with Ringo (right), Phil Spector (standing) and George Harrison playing guitar..

George Harrison sits at the steel guitar during at the Abbey Road studio with Pete (left) Ringo and Billy Preston with Peter Frampton, seated..

Paul McCartney and Chet Atkins at Chet's home in Nashville. (Photo courtesy of Merle Russell)

Paul and Leona Atkins during Paul's time in Nashville in 1974. (Photo courtesy of Merle Russell)

Paul McCartney and Leona Atkins in Nashville. (Photo courtesy of Merle Russell)

On the back of the picture of Paul and Leona Atkins, Paul wrote this to Merle Atkins Russell. The baby mentioned on the bottom is my son, Jonathan. Paul and Linda were kind enough to send me flowers when he was born a few days later. (Photo courtesy of Merle Russell)

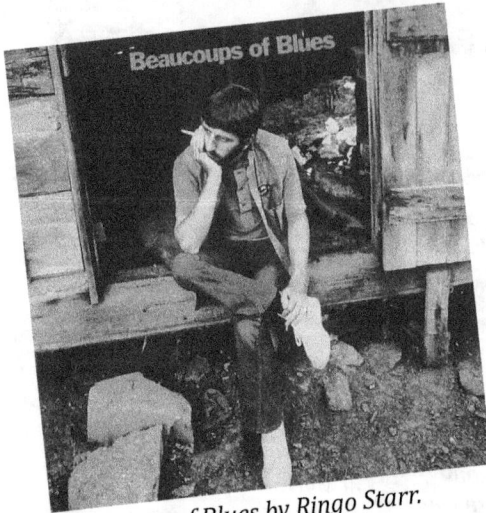

Beaucoups of Blues by Ringo Starr.

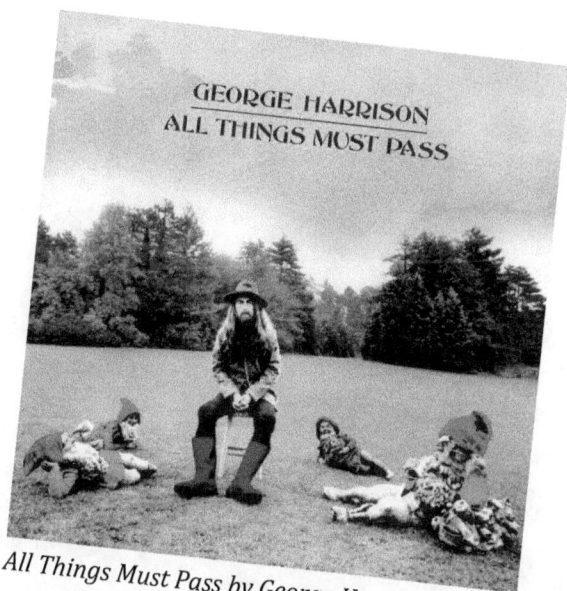

All Things Must Pass by George Harrison.

George and Pete at steel.
(Photo courtesy of Rose Drake)

WORKS CITED

Introduction

1. Information from *Discovering Country Music* by Don Cusic. (Praeger, *2008*)

Beatles and Country Music Fans Surprised

1. Lewisohn, Mark. *Tune In: The Beatles: All These Years.* New York: Crown Archetype, 2013.p. 48 and Clayson, Alan. *Ringo Starr.* London: MPG Books, 1996, 2003. P. 38-31; Beatles Anthology p. 35.
2. Beatles *Anthology*, p. 36.
3. Beatles *Anthology*, p. 36.
4. Beatles *Anthology*, p. 107.
5. Display in Beatles Museum, Liverpool, England.
6. Beatles *Anthology*, p. 27.
7. Louise Harrison interview, October, 31, 2014.

Slim Whitman

1. All information on British Charts comes from Guinness Book
2. Lewisohn, Mark. *Tune In:* p. 81; Beatles *Anthology*, p. 27.
3. Lewisohn, Mark. *Tune In:* p. 135; Sounes, Howard. *Fab: An Intimate Life of Paul McCartney.* New York: Da Capo Press, 2010, p. 7.
4. Beatles *Anthology*, p. 11l Lewisohn, Mark. *Tune In:* p. 49.
5. Beatles *Anthology*, p. 80; Lewisohn, Mark. *Tune In:* p. 80

Skiffle

1. Spitz, Bob. *The Beatles: The Biography.* New York: Little, Brown and Company, 2005. P. 44
2. Sounes, p. 18.

Lonnie Donegan

1. Cohen, Ronald and Rachel Clare Donaldson. *Roots of the Revival: American & British Folk Music in the 1950s.* Urbana: University of Illinois Press, 2014, p 62.
2. Personally observed by me on visits to the British Sound museum when it was at the O2 Center in London.

Rock Island Line

1. All references to the American charts come from the Joel Whitburn books All information on American charts comes from the Joel Whitburn books: Whitburn, Joel. *Hot Country Songs, 1944 to 2008.* Menomonee Falls, Wisconsin: Record Research, Inc. 2008; Whitburn, Joel. *Hot Country Songs, 1944 to 2008.* Menomonee Falls, Wisconsin: Record Research, Inc. 2008; Whitburn, Joel. *The Billboard Albums,* 6th Edition. Menomonee Falls, Wisconsin: Record Research, Inc. 2006; Whitburn, Joel. *Top Pop Singles,* 12th Edition. Menomonee Falls, Wisconsin: Record Research, Inc. 2008.
2. Norman, Philip. *Shout! The Beatles in Their Generation.* New York: MJF Books, 1981, p. 40.
3. Beatles *Anthology,* p. 28.

Skiffle and Country Music in Liverpool

1. Beatles *Anthology,* p. 10.
2. Clayson, *Ringo* pp. 30-31
3. Clayson, Alan. *George Harrison.* London: MPG Books, 1996, 2003, p. 34.
4. Lewisohn, Tune In, pp 48-49.
5. Conversation with Mark Hagen, Executive Producer, BBC, July 22, 2013.

Bill Haley and The Comets

1. Information on Bill Haley from Swenson, John. *Bill Haley: The Daddy of Rock and Roll.* New York: Stein and Day, 1983.

Elvis Presley

1. Information from Elvis and Nashville by Don Cusic (Nashville: Brackish, 2012.

Carl Perkins, The Everly Brothers and Jerry Lee Lewis

1. Lewisohn, Mark. *Tune In:* p. 91.

Buddy Holly

1. Information from Amburn, Ellis. *Buddy Holly: A Biography.* New York: St. Martin's Press, 1995.
2. Beatles *Anthology*, p.22.
3. Lewisohn, Tune In, 146, 149.

Country Influences on the Young Beatles

1. Beatles *Anthology*, p. 11-12.
2. Lewisohn, Tune In, p. 81.

From Skiffle to Rockabilly

1. Beatles *Anthology*, p. 21; Lewisohn, Tune In, p. 110.

Influential Rock and Roll Records

1. Lewisohn, Mark. *Tune In:* p. 287.

The Beatles On The BBC

1. Howlett, Kevin. *The Beatles: The BBC Archives: 1962-1970.* New York: Harper Design, 2013, p. 18

The Beatles First Professional British Recordings

1. Interview with Paul McCartney in Lewisohn, Mark. *The Complete Beatles Recording Sessions.* New York: Metro Books, 1988.
2. Lewisohn, Mark. *The Complete Beatles Chronicle.* New York: Harmony Books, 1992, p. 99.

Country Roots of Beatles Guitars

1. Thomson, Graeme. *Behind the Locked Door: George Harrison.* London: Overlook and Omnibus Press, 2015, p. 21.
2. Thomson, PAGE NUMBER!!!
3. Lewisohn, Mark. *Tune In:* p. 150.

Gretsch Guitars

1. Lewisohn, Mark. *Tune In:* p. 150.
2. Babiuk, Andy. Beatles Gear. Milwaukee: Backbeat Books, 2001, 2002, p. 31; Lewisohn, Mark. *Tune In:* p.369.
3. Lewisohn, Mark. *Tune In:* p. 464-465; Beatles *Anthology*, p. 81; Babiuk, p. 31.
4. Beatles *Anthology*, p. 81.
5. Lewisohn, Tune In, p. 465.
6. Lewisohn, Tune In, p. 465.
7. Babiuk, p. 53.

Chet Atkins and Gretsch Guitars

1. Information from Atkins, Chet. *Me and My Guitars*. Milwaukee: Hal Leonard, 2001, 2004.
2. Carl Perkins in England
3. Perkins, Carl and David McGee. *Go, Cat Go!: The Life and Times of Carl Perkins*. New York: Hyperion, 1996, p 295.
4. Carl Perkins Meets The Beatles
5. Perkins, p. 297.
6. Perkins, p. 298-299.

Beatle Guitars & Country Music

1. Information from Cusic. Don. "Guitars, Cowboys and Country Music" in *The Cowboy In Country Music: An Historical Survey with Artist Profiles*. Jefferson, N.C.: McFarland and Company, 2011.

The Beatles and the Singing Cowboys

1. Information from Pando, Leo. *The Illustrated History of Trigger: The Lives and Legend of Roy Rogers' Palomino*. Jefferson, N.C.: McFarland & Company, Inc., 2007)

Rickenbacker

1. Beatles *Anthology*, p. 81.

The Beatles and Gibson Guitars

1. Babiuk, p. 51.
2. Babiuk, p. 72.

George Harrison's American Visit

1. Harrison, Olivia. *Living in the Material World.* New York: Abrams, 2011, p. 115.
2. Kirkpatrick, Jim. *Before He Was Fab: George Harrison's First American Visit.* Vienna, ILL: Cache River Press, 2000, p. 17.
3. Kirkpatrick, p. 22.
4. Kirkpatrick, p. 26.
5. Kirkpatrick, p. 29.
6. Beatles *Anthology*, p. 116.
7. Kirkpatrick, p. 34.
8. Kirkpatrick, p. 37.

The Gretsch Country Gentleman and Tennessean

1. Babiuk, p. 105.

Rickenbacker 12 String

1. Babiuk, p. 110-111.
2. Babiuk, p. 113.
3. Pritcher, Mark. "An Interview with Steve Wariner" in Mister Guitar, Issue 38, June 1996, p. 5.

Hard Day's Night

1. Babiuk, p.119.

Gretsch 12 String

1. Babiuk, p. 148.
2. "Ask Chet" in Mister Guitar, Issue No. 3, November, 1983.

The Beatles and Epiphone Guitars

1. Babiuk, p. 152.

The Beatles and Fender Guitars

1. Babiuk, p. 157.
2. Beatles Anthology, p. 81.
3. Emerick, Geoff with Howard Massey. *Here, There and Everywhere: My Life Recording the Music of the Beatles.* New York: Gotham Books, 2006, p. 107.
4. Beatles Anthology, p. 18.

Act Naturally

1. Interview with Paul McCartney in Lewisohn, Mark. *The Complete Beatles Recording Sessions.* New York: Metro Books, 1988, p. 12.
2. MacDonald, Ian. *Revolution in the Head: The Beatles' Records and the Sixties.* Third Edition. Chicago: Chicago Review Press, 2005, p. 160.

Ken Mansfield and The Beatles

1. Mansfield, Ken with Brent Stoker. *The White Book: the Beatles, the Bands, the Biz: An Insider's Look at an Era.* Nashville: Thomas Nelson, 2007, p. 41.
2. Mansfield, Ken. Personal interview, February 25, 2015.

Nashville Sessions

1. Martin, George with Jeremy Hornsby. *All You Need Is Ears.* New York: St. Martin's Press, 1979, p. 132.
2. Martin, "All You Need is Ears," p. 133.
3. Babiuk, p. 162.
4. James, Gary. "Interview with Superstar Picker Norbert Putnam" in www.classicbands.com

Fuzz Tone

1. Cooper, Peter. How a happy accident revolutionized guitar sound." *Nashville Tennessean*, August 4, 2013

The Lost Gretsch

1. Babiuk, p. 174-175.

Country Shipments to Ringo

1. Mansfield, Ken. Personal interview, February 25, 2015.

Revolver

1. Babiuk, p. 182.

The Gibson J-200

1. "Ray Whitley" in The Cowboy in Country Music by Don Cusic, p. 51-52.

The Nashville Invasion

1. Harrison, George. Liner notes to *Chet Atkins: Picks on the Beatles*, RCA LPM 3531 and LSP 3551, 1966.

Paul is Dead Story & The Country Connection

1. Cusic, Don. *It's the Cowboy Way!: The Amazing True Adventures of Riders In The Sky*. Lexington: University Press of Kentucky, 2003.

Ringo's Sentimental Journey

1. Horstman, Dorothy. *Sing Your Heart Out, Country Boy*. New York: E.P. Dutton & Co., Inc., 1975, p. 123.

The Beatles and Bob Dylan

1. Spitz, Bob. *The Beatles: The Biography*. New York: Little, Brown and Company, 2005, p. 533.

Dylan in Nashville

1. Chambers, Joe. Personal interview, January 9, 2015.
2. Daniels, Charlie and Bebe Evans. Daniels relayed this to me through Bebe on June 2, 2015; he also told the story to Eddie Stubbs during an interview on WSM on June 1, 2015.
3. Cooper, Peter. "Music erases all differences for Daniels: Legend embraces past with Bob Dylan in new album. *The Nashville Tennessean*, March 30, 2014, 7E, 8E.

George Harrison and Pete Drake

1. Drake, Rose. Interview by author, March 31, 2014.
2. Shelton, Robert. *No Direction Home: The Life and Music of Bob Dylan.* New York: Beech Tree Books/William Morrow, 1986, p 408.

Beaucoups of Blues

1. Moore, Scotty as told to James Dickerson. *That's Alright, Elvis: The Untold Story of Elvis's First Guitarist and Manager, Scotty Moore.* New York: Schirmer Books, 1997, p. 70.
2. Wyatt, Eugene. "Ringo Starr Hits Town On the Sly," *Nashville Tennessean*, June 24, 1970, p. 1, 6.)
3. Drake interview.
4. Picture, *Nashville Banner*, June 30, 1970.
5. Wyatt, Gene. "'Country Ringo' Breezes Through A Quick Sessions." *Nashville Tennessean*, June 27, 1970, p. 1, 8.

Ringo's Songs With The Beatles

1. Emerick, p. 104.
2. Emerick, p. 118.
3. Davies, Hunter, ed. *The Beatles Lyrics*. New York: Little, Brown & Co. 2014, p. 287, 343.
4. Beatles Anthology, p. 306.

Ringo During the Nashville Sessions

1. Evans, Mac interview July 24, 2014.
2. Emerick, p. 245.
3. Moore, p. 192-193.
4. Evans interview.

Marshall Fallwell: Rock Photographer

1. Fallwell, Marshall, personal interview, August 29, 2014.

George's Note to Pete

1. Drake, Rose and Joe Chambers with Musicians Hall of Fame.

Norbert Putnam and David Briggs

1. James, Gary. "Interview with Superstar Picker Norbert Putnam" in www.classicbands.com
2. James.

Marshall Fallwell: Rock Photographer

1. Fallwell interview.

America in 1970

1. Gallup, George. "War Disillusionment Is High," *Nashville Banner*, June 28, 1970.
2. Fritchey, Clayton. "Number 1 Problem' Doesn't Make Sense, *Nashville Banner*, June 26, 1970. "It Is Time For Us Americans To Check our Stitches," Graham Says." Nashville Banner, July 6, 1970.
3. "It's Time For Us." "Georgia Pop Festival Blares 'Disgrace' Note. *Nashville Banner*, July 6, 1970.
4. "Georgia Pop Festival Blares 'Disgrace' Note. Nashville Banner, July 6, 1970.

Hair

1. Beatles Anthology, p. 119.
2. Buckley, William. "Long Hair: A Symbol of the Exhibitionist," *Nashville Banner*, July 1, 1970.
3. West, Morris. "An Old Man and Long Hair," *Nashville Banner*, July 4, 1970.
4. Blydstone, Richard. "About That Rug On Your Neck, Pal," A.P. *Nashville Banner*, July 5, 1970.

Gary Burr and Gary Nicholson

1. Burr, Gary. Email to author, November 25, 2014.
2. Richard Courtney interview of Gary Burr on WHPY in Nashville.

Paul McCartney in Nashville

1. O'Donnell, Red. "McCartney Here For Five Weeks." *The Nashville Banner*, June 7, 1974, p. 17.

2. Bailey, Jerry and Eve Zibart. "McCartney in Nashville for 3 Rs." *The Tennessean*, June 7, 1974, p. 1, 12.

3. Bailey, Jerry and Eve Zibart. "McCartney in Nashville for 3 Rs." *The Tennessean*, June 7, 1974, p. 1, 12

4. O'Donnell, Red. "McCartney Here For Five Weeks." *The Nashville Banner*, June 7, 1974, p. 17.

5. Swingley, Pat. "Linda McCartney: The Woman At Paul's Side." *The Tennessean*, July 21, 1974, p. 1E, 11.

The McCartneys At Opryland

1. Walker, Irene. "McCartney Visit Adds To Contest." *The Tennessean*, June 17, 1974.

2. Hance, Bill. "McCartneys Draw Squeals at Opryland." *The Nashville Banner*, June 17, 1974, p. 17.

3. Killen, Buddy with Tom Carter. *By The Seat of My Pants: My Life in Country Music*. New York: Simon & Schuster, 1993, p. 215.

4. Killen, p. 216.

The McCartney Sessions

1. Winfrey, Ernie. Personal interview, July 28, 2014.

Sally G.

1. Green, Lloyd. Personal interview, September 1, 2014.

2. Green, Lloyd. Oral history interview at the Country Music Foundation.

Hey Diddle

1. Winfrey interview.

Lloyd Green on "Hey Diddle"

1. Green, personal interview.

Chet Atkins and Paul

1. Pritcher, Mark. "Chet Atkins and the Beatles" in *Mister Guitar*, Issue 34, Winter 1995.

Paul & Chet & The Country Hams

1. Pritcher, Mark. "Walking in the Park with Eloise Part II." From an interview with Paul McCartney for Mike Read with the BBC in Mister Guitar, Issue 34, March, 1955.

Junior's Farm

1. Winfrey interview.

Linda and Dixie

1. Gamble, Dixie, personal interview August 27, 2014.

Bobby Braddock

1. Braddock, Bobby, personal email, September 29, 2014.

Dixie's Party

1. Gamble interview.

Jimmy McCulloch

1. Winfrey interview.

Linda and Paul

1. Gamble interview.

Danny Ealey: Super Fan

1. Ealey, Danny. Personal interview, August 29, 2014.

The McCartneys Visit Johnny Cash

1. Interview with John Carter Cash, May 29, 2015.
2. Bailey, Jerry. "Paul & Linda Try the Gentle Life." *The Tennessean*, July 18, 1974, p. 67, 70.

Saying Good-Bye to Nashville

1. Bailey, Jerry. "Paul and Linda Try the Gentle Life," *Nashville Tennessean*, July 18, 1974.

Leaving Nashville

1. Gamble interview.

Lloyd Green With Paul in France

1. Green, personal interview.

Lloyd Green and Paul—The Last Session

1. Green, personal interview.

Linda McCartney

1. Green, personal interview.

Good-bye, John

1. Mansfield, The White Book, p. 87.
2. Norbert Putnam, David Briggs and George Harrison
3. Norbert Putnam, personal interview June 3, 2015.

A Letter From Paul to Lloyd Green

1. Green, personal interview.

Waylon and Ringo

1. Mansfield, *The White Book*, p. 183.
2. Mansfield, personal interview.

New Moon Over Jamaica

1. Interview with John Carter Cash, May 29, 2015.

Larry Hosford & George Harrison

1. www.larryhosford.net

Ringo and Dolly Parton

1. Mansfield, *The White Book*, p. 183-184.

Act Naturally Redux

1. Sisk, Eileen. *Buck Owens: The Biography*. Chicago: Chicago Review Press, 2010. P. 286-287.
2. Owens, Buck with Randy Poe. *Buck 'Em!: The Autobiography of Buck Owens*. Milwaukee: Backbeat Books (Hal Leonard), 2013. P. 288.

Ringo Thirty-eight Years Later

1. Ghianni, Tim. Nashville Starr: When Ringo Came to Town. *Nashville Scene*, July 3, 2008.

Beatle Songs in Country Music

1. Beatles *Anthology*, p. 160.

Epilogue

1. *Melody Maker* Nov 14, 1965.
2. Paul McCartney interview in Lewisohn, Mark. *The Complete Beatles Recording Sessions*. New York: Metro Books, 1988, p. 7.
3. Cason, Buzz. Conversation, November 29, 2014.
4. McCartney interview in Lewisohn, Mark. *The Complete Beatles Recording Sessions*. New York: Metro Books, 1988, p. 8.
5. Martin, *All You Need is Ears*, p. 132.
6. Clayson, *Ringo*, p. 206.

BIBLIOGRAPHY

Amburn, Ellis. *Buddy Holly: A Biography*. New York: St. Martin's Press, 1995.

Amburn, Ellis. *Dark Star: The Roy Orbison Story*. New York: A Lyle Stuart Book published by Carol Publishing Group, 1990.

Ask Chet," in *Mister Guitar*, Issue No. 3, November, 1983.

Atkins, Chet with Bill Neely. *Country Gentleman*. Chicago: Henry Regnery Company, 1974.

Atkins, Chet. *Me and My Guitars*. Milwaukee: Hal Leonard, 2001, 2004.

Babiuk, Andy. *Beatles Gear*. Milwaukee: Backbeat Books, 2001, 2002.

Babiuk, Andy. *The Story of Paul Bigsby: Father of the Modern Electric Solidbody Guitar*. Savannah, GA: FG Publishing, 2008.

Bacon, Tony. *50 Years of Gretsch Electrics*. New York: Backbeat Books, 2005.

Bacon, Tony. *The Fender Electric Guitar Book: A Complete History of Fender Instruments*. New York: Backbeat, 1992, 1998, 2007.

Bacon, Tony. *The History of the American Guitar: From 1833 to the Present Day*. New York: Outline Press, Ltd, 2001.

Bailey, Jerry and Eve Zibart. "McCartney in Nashville for 3 Rs." *The Tennessean*, June 7, 1974.

Bailey, Jerry. "Beatle Fans Take Heart: Paul McCartney Plans Social Life While Here." *The Tennessean*.

Bailey, Jerry. "Paul and Linda Try the Gentle Life," *Nashville Tennessean*, July 18, 1974.

Beatles, The. Anthology. San Francisco: Chronicle Books, 2000.

Blydstone, Richard. "About That Rug On Your Neck, Pal," A.P. *Nashville Banner*, July 5, 1970.

Braddock, Bobby, personal email, September 29, 2014.

Bronson, Fred. *The Billboard Book of Number One Hits: The Inside Story Behind the Top of the Charts*. New York: Billboard Publications, 1985.

Brooks, Tim and Earle Marsh. *The Complete Directory to Prime Time Network and Cable TV Shows 1946-Present*. New York: Ballantine Books, 1978, 1981, 1985, 1988, 1992, 1995, 2003.

Buckley, William. "Long Hair: A Symbol of the Exhibitionist," *Nashville Banner*, July 1, 1970.

Burke, Ken and Dan Griffin. *The Blue Moon Boys: The Story of Elvis Presley's Band*. Chicago: Chicago Review Press, 2006.

Burr, Gary. Interviewed by Richard Courtney on WHPY radio in Nashville.

Burr, Gary. Email to author, November 25, 2014.

Carter, Walter. *Gibson Guitars: 100 Years of an American Icon*. Nashville: Gibson Publishing, 1994.

Carter, Walter. *The Gibson Electric Guitar Book: Seventy Years of Classic Guitars*. New York: Backbeat Books, 2007.

Casdorph, Paul D. *Let the Good Times Roll: Life at Home in America During WWII*. New York: Paragon House, 1989.

Cash, John Carter. Personal interview, May 29, 2015.

Castleman, Harry and Walter J. Podrazik. *All Together Now: The First Complete Beatles Discography 1961-1975*. New York: Ballantine, 1975.

Chambers, Joe. Personal interview, January 9, 2015.

Chapman, Richard. *Guitar: Music, History, Players*. New York: Dorling Kindersley, 2000.

Clayson, Alan. *George Harrison*. London: MPG Books, 1996, 2003

Clayson, Alan. *John Lennon*. London: MPG Books, 2003

Clayson, Alan. *Paul McCartney*. London: MPG Books, 2003

Clayson, Alan. *Ringo Starr*. London: MPG Books, 1996, 2003. P. 20

Cohen, Ronald and Rachel Clare Donaldson. *Roots of the Revival: American & British Folk Music in the 1950s*. Urbana: University of Illinois Press, 2014.

Cooper, Peter. "How a happy accident revolutionized guitar sound." *Nashville Tennessean*, August 4, 2013

Cooper, Peter. "Music erases all differences for Daniels: Legend embraces past with Bob Dylan in new album. *The Nashville Tennessean*, March 30, 2014.

Cusic, Don. *Discovering Country Music*. Westport, CT: Praeger, 2008.

Cusic, Don. Elvis and Nashville. Nashville: Brackish, 2012.

Cusic, Don. *Elvis in Nashville*. Nashville: Brackish, 2012.

Cusic, Don. *Gene Autry: His Life and Career*. Jefferson, N.C.: McFarland and Company, 2007.

Cusic, Don. *It's the Cowboy Way!: The Amazing True Adventures of Riders In The Sky*. Lexington: University Press of Kentucky, 2003.

Cusic, Don. *Roger Miller: Dang Him!* Nashville: Brackish,2012.

Cusic. Don. *The Cowboy In Country Music: An Historical Survey with Artist Profiles.* Jefferson, N.C.: McFarland and Company, 2011.

Darnell, Catherine. "Poor Paul." *The Tennessean,* May 10, 1997, p. 1-D

Davies, Hunter, ed. The Beatles Lyrics. New York: Little, Brown & Co. 2014.

Davies, Hunter. *The Beatles: The Authorized Biography Updated.* New York: W.W. Norton and Company, 1968, 1978, 1985, 2002, 2009.

Demain, Bill. "When We Was Fab: Nashvillians remember Paul McCartney and Wings' working vacation here in 1974." *Nashville Scene,* April 18, 2002.

Drake, Rose. Interview by author, March 31, 2014.

Ealey, Danny. Personal interview, August 29, 2014.

Emerick, Geoff with Howard Massey. *Here, There and Everywhere: My Life Recording the Music of the Beatles.* New York: Gotham Books, 2006.

Evans, Mac interview July 24, 2014

Evans, Steve and Ron Middlebrook. *Cowboy Guitars.* Jacksonville, Arkansas: Centerstream, Publishing, 2009.

Fallwell, Marshall, personal interview, August 29, 2014.

Fritchey, Clayton. "Number 1 Problem' Doesn't Make Sense, *Nashville Banner,* June 26, 1970.

Gallup, George. "War Disillusionment Is High," *Nashville Banner,* June 28, 1970.

Gamble, Dixie. Personal interview August 27, 2014.

Georgia Pop Festival Blares 'Disgrace' Note. Nashville Banner, July 6, 1970. Gallup, George. "War Disillusionment Is High," Nashville Banner, June 28, 1970.

Georgia Pop Festival Blares 'Disgrace' Note." *Nashville Banner,* July 6, 1970.

Ghianni, Tim. "McCartney's return fulfills old promise." *Westview Newspaper,* Vol 34, No. 29, July 23-29, 2010.

Ghianni, Tim. Nashville Starr: When Ringo Came to Town. *Nashville Scene,* July 3, 2008.

Giulano, Geoffrey. *Dark Horse: The Life and Art of George Harrison.* New York: DaCapo Press, 1997.

Gould, Jonathan. *Can't Buy Me Love: The Beatles, Britain, and America.* New York: Harmony Books, 2007.

Green, Lloyd. Personal interview, September 1, 2014.

Green, Lloyd. Oral history interview at the Country Music Foundation.

Greene, Joshua. *Here Comes the Sun: The Spiritual and Musical Journey of George Harrison*. Hoboken, N.J.: John Wiley & Sons, 2006.

Gruhn, George and Walter Carter. "Gibson Super 400." *Vintage Guitar* magazine, September 16, 2009.

Gruhn, George. "Stromberg Master 400." *Vintage Guitar* magazine, December 1, 2005.

Guralnick, Peter. *Carless Love: The Unmaking of Elvis Presley*. Boston: Little, Brown and Company, 1999.

Guralnick, Peter. *Last Train to Memphis: The Rise of Elvis Presley*. Boston: Little, Brown and Company, 1994.

Hance, Bill. "McCartneys Draw Squeals at Opryland." *The Nashville Banner*, June 17, 1974, p. 17

Harrison, George. *I, Me, Mine*. San Francisco: Chronicle Books, 1980, 2002.

Harrison, George. Liner notes to *Chet Atkins: Picks on the Beatles*, RCA LPM 3531 and LSP 3551, 1966.

Harrison, Louise. Personal interview, October 31, 2014.

Harrison, Olivia. *Living in the Material World*. New York: Abrams, 2011.

Hertsgaard, Mark. *A Day In The Life: The Music and Artistry of the Beatles*. New York: Delacorte Press, 1996.

Hilburn, Robert. *Johnny Cash: The Life*. Boston: Little, Brown and Company, 2013.

Horstman, Dorothy. *Sing Your Heart Out, Country Boy*. New York: E.P. Dutton & Co., Inc., 1975.

Hosford, Larry web site: www.larryhosford.net

Howlett, Kevin. *The Beatles: The BBC Archives: 1962-1970*. New York: Harper Design, 2013.

"It Is Time For Us Americans To Check our Stitches,' Graham Says." *Nashville Banner*, July 6, 1970.

James, Gary. "Interview with Superstar Picker Norbert Putnam" in www.classicbands.com

Johnston, Richard and Dick Boak. *Martin Guitars: A History*. New York: Hal Leonard, 1988, 1994, 2008.

Killen, Buddy with Tom Carter. *By The Seat of My Pants: My Life in Country Music*. New York: Simon & Schuster, 1993.

Kirkpatrick, Jim. *Before He Was Fab: George Harrison's First American Visit*. Vienna, ILL: Cache River Press, 2000.

Labour, Fred. Author interview, January 12, 2014.

Lawrence, Alistair. *Abbey Road Studios: The Best Studio in the World*. London: Bloomsbury, 2012.

Lee, Brenda with Robert K. Oermann and Julie Clay. *Little Miss Dynamite: The Life and Times of Brenda Lee*. New York: Hyperion, 2002.

Leng, Simon. *While My Guitar Gently Weeps: The Music of George Harrison*. Milwaukee: Hal Leonard, 2006.

Lewisohn, Mark. *The Complete Beatles Chronicle*. New York: Harmony Books, 1992.

Lewisohn, Mark. *The Complete Beatles Recording Sessions*. New York: Metro Books, 1988.

Lewisohn, Mark. *Tune In: The Beatles: All These Years*. New York: Crown Archetype, 2013.

Love, Robert and Editors of Rolling Stone. *Harrison* (with Forward by Olivia Harrison). New York: Simon and Schuster, 2002.

MacDonald, Ian. *Revolution in the Head: The Beatles' Records and the Sixties*. Third Edition. Chicago: Chicago Review Press, 2005.

Mansfield, Ken. *The Beatles, The Bible and Bodega Bay: My Long and Winding Road*. Nashville, TN: Broadman & Holman, 2000.

Mansfield, Ken with Brent Stoker. *The White Book: the Beatles, the Bands, the Biz: An Insider's Look at an Era*. Nashville: Thomas Nelson, 2007

Mansfield, Ken. Personal interview, February 25, 2015.

Martin, George with Jeremy Hornsby. *All You Need Is Ears*. New York: St. Martin's Press, 1979.

Martin, George with William Pearson. *With a Little Help From My Friends: The Making of Sgt. Pepper*. Boston: Little, Brown & Company, 1994.

"McCartneys Wing Way Back Home. *Nashville Banner*, July 18, 1974, p. 21.

McKinney, Devin. *The Beatles In Dreams and History*. Cambridge, MA: Harvard University Press, 2003.

Miles, Barry. *Paul McCartney: Many Years From Now*. New York: Henry Holt and Company, 1997.

Moore, Scotty as told to James Dickerson. *That's Alright, Elvis: The Untold Story of Elvis's First Guitarist and Manager, Scotty Moore*. New York: Schirmer Books, 1997.

Norman, Philip. *John Lennon: The Life*. New York: Ecco, 2008.

Norman, Philip. *Shout! The Beatles in Their Generation*. New York: MJF Books, 1981.

O'Donnell, Red. "Beatles' Paul McCartney 'Winging' His Way Here." *Nashville Banner*, May 23, 1974, p. 1

O'Donnell, Red. "McCartney Here For Five Weeks." *The Nashville Banner*, June 7, 1974.

Owens, Buck with Randy Poe. *Buck 'Em!: The Autobiography of Buck Owens*. Milwaukee: Backbeat Books (Hal Leonard), 2013

Pando, Leo. *The Illustrated History of Trigger: The Lives and Legend of Roy Rogers' Palomino*. Jefferson, N.C.: McFarland & Company, Inc., 2007)

Perkins, Carl and David McGee. *Go, Cat Go!: The Life and Times of Carl Perkins*. New York: Hyperion, 1996.

Pritchard, David and Alan Lysaght. *The Beatles: An Oral History*. New York: Hyperion, 1998.

Pritcher, Mark. "An Interview with Steve Wariner" in *Mister Guitar*, Issue 38, June 1996

Pritcher, Mark. "Ask Chet" in *Mister Guitar*, Issue No. 3, November, 1983.

Pritcher, Mark. "Chet Atkins and the Beatles" in *Mister Guitar*, Issue 34, Winter 1995.

Pritcher, Mark. "Walking in the Park with Eloise Part II." From an interview with Paul McCartney for Mike Read with the BBC in *Mister Guitar*, Issue 34, March, 1955.

Putnam, Norbert. Personal interview, June 3, 2015.

Ribowsky, Mark. *He's a Rebel: The Truth About Phil Spector—Rock and Roll's Legendary Madman*. New York: E.P. Dutton, 1989.

Roberts, David, editor. *British Hit Singles: Guinness World Records, 15th Edition*, edited by David Roberts. Great Britain: Guinness World Records Ltd, 2001. .

Shapiro, Marc. *Behind Sad Eyes: George Harrison*. New York: St. Martin's Press, 2002.

Shelton, Robert. *No Direction Home: The Life and Music of Bob Dylan*. Beech Tree/William Morrow, 1986.

Sisk, Eileen. *Buck Owens: The Biography*. Chicago: Chicago Review Press, 2010.

Sounes, Howard. *Fab: An Intimate Life of Paul McCartney*. New York: Da Capo Press, 2010.

Southall, Brian, Peter Vince, Allan Rouse. *Abbey Road.* London: Omnibus Press, 1982, 1997, 2002.

Spitz, Bob. *The Beatles: The Biography.* New York: Little, Brown and Company, 2005.

Starr, Michael Seth, Ringo: *With A Little Help.* New York: Backbeat/Hal Leonard, 2015.

Swenson, John. *Bill Haley: The Daddy of Rock and Roll.* New York: Stein and Day, 1983.

Swingley, Pat. "Linda McCartney: The Woman At Paul's Side." *The Tennessean,* July 21, 1974, p. 1E, 11E

Taylor, Derek. *It Was Twenty Years Ago Today.* New York: Simon & Schuster, 1987.

Thomson, Graeme. *Behind the Locked Door: George Harrison.* London: Overlook and Omnibus Press, 2015.

Tillery, Gary. *Working Class Mystic: A Spiritual Biography of George Harrison.* Wheaton, IL and Chennai, India: Theosophical Publishing House, 2011.

Trynka, Paul, editor. *The Electric Guitar: An Illustrated History.* San Francisco: Chronicle Books, 1993.

Turner, Steve. *A Hard Day's Write: The Stories Behind Every Beatles Song.* London: Carlton, 1994, 1999.

Wald, Elijah. *How the Beatles Destroyed Rock'N'roll: A Alternative History of American Popular Music.* New York: Oxford University Press, 2009.

Walker, Irene. "McCartney Visit Adds To Contest." *The Tennessean,* June 17, 1974.

West, Morris. "An Old Man and Long Hair," *Nashville Banner,* July 4, 1970.

Wheeler, Tom. *American Guitars: An Illustrated History: Revised and Updated.* New York: HarperCollins, 1992.

Whitburn, Joel. *Hot Country Songs: Billboard 1944-2008.* Menomonee Falls, Wisconsin, 2008.

Whitburn, Joel. *The Billboard Albums,* 6th Edition. Menomonee Falls, Wisconsin: Record Research, Inc. 2006.

Whitburn, Joel. *Top Pop Singles,* 12th Edition. Menomonee Falls, Wisconsin: Record Research, Inc. 2008.

White, Forrest. *The Fender Inside Story.* San Francisco: GPI Books, 1994.

Whitford, Eldon and David Vinopal. "Gibson SJ-200: On the Trail to the Original." *Vintage Guitar* magazine, August 10, 2004.

Whitford, Eldon, David Vinopal and Dan Erlewine. *Gibson's Fabulous Flat-Top Guitars: An Illustrated History & Guide*. New York: Backbeat Books, 1994, 2009.

Wiener, Allen J. *The Beatles: The Ultimate Recording Guide*. New York: Facts On File, 1986, 1992.

Winfrey, Ernie. Personal interview, July 28, 2014

Wright, Michael. "1,000 Years of the Guitar: A Contextual Reflection." *Vintage Guitar* magazine, July 5, 2001.

Wright, Michael. "Harmony: The Parlor Years (1892-1914)." *Vintage Guitar* magazine, January 7, 2002.

Wright, Michael. "Supertone Gene Autry Roundup 1938." *Vintage Guitar* magazine, January 27, 2005.

Wyatt, Eugene. "Ringo Starr Hits Town On the Sly," Nashville Tennessean, June 24, 1970, p. 1, 6.)

Wyatt, Gene. "'Country Ringo' Breezes Through A Quick Sessions." Nashville Tennessean, June 27, 1970, p. 1, 8.

Younger, Richard. *Get a Shot of Rhythm & Blues: The Arthur Alexander Story*. Tuscaloosa: University of Alabama Press, 2000.

INDEX

www.ingramcontent.com/pod-product-compliance
Lightning Source LLC
LaVergne TN
LVHW051459080426
835509LV00017B/1826